La Belle *Cuisine*

Broadway Books • New York • New York • Broadway Books

Patti LaBelle

with Laura B. Randolph

LaBelle Cuisine

Recipes to *Sing* About

BROADWAY

Broadway Books titles may be purchased for business or
promotional use or for special sales. For information, please
write to: Special Markets Department, Random House, Inc.,
1540 Broadway, New York, NY 10036.

BROADWAY BOOKS and its logo, a letter B bisected on the
diagonal, are trademarks of Broadway Books, a division of
Random House, Inc.

Visit our website at www.broadwaybooks.com

Library of Congress Cataloging-in-Publication Data
LaBelle, Patti.
      LaBelle cuisine : recipes to sing about / Patti LaBelle with
   Laura B. Randolph.
          p.   cm.
      Includes index.
      ISBN 0-7679-0314-5
      1. Cookery, American.   I. Randolph, Laura B.
   II. Title.
      TX715.L127   1999   98-49145
      641.5973—dc21   CIP

FIRST EDITION

Designed by Judith Stagnitto Abbate /ABBATE DESIGN

      02   03   20   19

This book is dedicated to all the cooks who have come before me who practiced and perfected this ancient healing art we call cooking. To them, I offer my heartfelt gratitude for showing me the true magic of meals: that how we prepare and present them nourishes the spirit as much as the stomach. And the most important ingredient of any recipe is love.

Contents

To-Die-For Desserts and Breads   159

Acknowledgments

To my aunts Hattie Mae Sibley and Joshia Mae James, my mother-in-law, Anna Edwards, and my forever friends, Norma Harris Gordon and Naomi Thompson: Thank you for walking me through the best, most beloved recipes of my ancestors and sharing so many of yours.

To Harriet Bell, for whom I have just two words: dream editor.

To Rick Rodgers, whose patience, professionalism, and passion for his work made what could have been a difficult project a delight.

To Al Lowman, thank you for your expertise, encouragement, and always enlightening advice.

And last but not least, a very special thank-you to Laura B. Randolph, who hears my voice in ways that continue to amaze me and captures it with style and grace for the printed page.

Introduction

From the time I was a little girl, I knew there were two things in this world I was born to do: sing and cook. I've spent my life developing my voice and my recipes and, to tell you the truth, I'm hard pressed to say where I'm happiest—in concert or in the kitchen; making music or making meals. Whether cooking or singing, I feel at ease, at peace, at one with the world.

While reminiscing for this book, I realized why cooking has always been such a labor of love for me. Because it's as much about friendship and fellowship as it is about food. Because, behind the whole process—the shopping, the planning, the preparing, the serving—cooking is really about love. Cooking is a way to show it, share it, serve it. Cooking is as much about nourishment for the soul as it is the stomach.

Especially the kind of cooking I grew up on. We're talking Southern, country cooking. Authentic, down-home, Southern country cooking is a generation-to-generation pass-it-down gift, and I have so many people in my family to thank for mine: my grandmothers, my mother, my father, my aunts Hattie Mae and Joshia Mae. I don't mean to brag, but the people in my family have always been some cooking folks. And that's no idle boast.

Do you know that, to this day, people still talk about my Grandmother Tempie's biscuits? And, let me tell you, that is high praise when you consider that at the time she was making them she was living on a farm in Piston, Georgia, where everybody, and I do mean *everybody* could cook. Especially the Sisters. A

xiii

Sister in Piston saying you could cook would be like Maya Angelou saying you could write.

But let me get back to those biscuits. When my father was a little boy, he couldn't get enough of his mother's biscuits. Whenever Grandmother Tempie baked a batch, he would park himself at the big kitchen table and eat a dozen biscuits at a time. And Daddy wasn't the only one who had a jones for those biscuits. People would come from miles around just on a *chance* they'd get to taste one. My Aunt Hattie Mae says Grandmother Tempie's biscuits were so light they could fly. And people swore that one day, one biscuit actually did.

Now, I can't vouch for the truth of the story, but I do know this: Folks used to eat an entire biscuit at once—just pick up the whole thing and stuff it in their mouth—ever since what people who were there that day refer to as The Incident. It happened at a Fourth of July picnic, and a whole bunch of folks say they saw it: the flying biscuit. As the story goes, one of Grandmother Tempie's neighbors was eating one of her biscuits when he set it down to reach for a glass of lemonade. It didn't take long—maybe fifteen, twenty seconds tops. But it was twenty seconds too long, because when he went to pick the biscuit back up, it was gone. Legend has it, while he was sipping his lemonade, that biscuit just floated away.

I feel so blessed that, before Grandmother Tempie got sick, she taught my father almost all of her secret recipes. Aunt Hattie Mae says Daddy practically lived in the kitchen with her. After school, all the other kids would head outside to play, but not Daddy. He'd stay right in the kitchen with Grandmother Tempie soaking up all her cooking secrets. Years later, growing up in Philly, I did the very same thing. Until I was 12, I spent hours at a time in my mother's kitchen. Where I grew up, in the closely knit, working-class community of Elmwood, out by the airport, there was a park right across the street from our house on South 84th Street where all the neighborhood kids used to play. All of them, that is, but me. All I wanted to do was hang out in the kitchen.

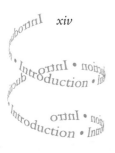

My mother and her best friend, my adopted Aunt Naomi, would offer to pay me to get me to go outside. Fifty cents apiece was the going rate. Some days the bribes worked, but most days they didn't, and, like Daddy, I would spend most of my free time sitting at our kitchen table watching as my mother and Naomi cooked up another mouthwatering meal. And, oh Lord, the dishes they would make! Fried chicken and fried corn. Barbecue pork smothered in barbecue sauce. Hot ribs and hot rolls. Greens, grits, and go-tell-it-on-the-mountain good gravy.

Thanks to Grandmother Tempie, my father knew his way around a kitchen, too. When my sisters and I were little, every morning before school, he would fix our braids and our breakfast. Whatever we wanted—pancakes and sausage, grits and eggs—Daddy would make for us. I don't know if we loved eating those breakfasts or Daddy loved cooking them for us more.

Daddy loved cooking so much that, before he got sick, he opened two restaurants, one in Harrisburg, Pennsylvania, called "The Broadway" and the other, "Baby Henry's Place," back home in Georgia. His customers in both places always said the same thing: They didn't know which was better, Daddy's food or Daddy's stories. He always put a lot of spice in both.

In the summer, he would buy a whole pig, dig a hole in the middle of the backyard, and roast the pig to golden-brown perfection. While everybody waited for it to get done, Chubby—that's what everybody called my mother—would pass around pitchers of homemade ice tea. When she poured Daddy's glass, he'd wink at his buddies and say: "I like my tea like I like my women: sweet, brown, and good to the last drop."

Had Grandmother Tempie lived to see him cooking in his restaurants, I know she would have been proud. I never even got to meet her; she died of leukemia when she was only 33. But there's one thing I know for sure and for certain, and I believe in my heart that my grandmother knew it, too. When she was in the kitchen cooking, she wasn't just making her family's meals, she was making their

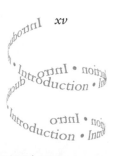

memories. She wasn't just blending spices, she was blending generations. And every time she heaped food on a plate, she heaped love on a person.

That's why I wrote this cookbook. To heap as much love on as many people as I can. To carry on Grandmother Tempie's tradition. To say thank you to my family, my friends, and my fans for the priceless gifts they have given me: the love, the laughter, the light that got me through my darkest days.

It's why I decided to share so many of my ancestors' treasured recipes—my mother's candied sweet potatoes (luscious), my father's bread pudding (legendary), Grandmother Tempie's flying biscuits (like nothing you have ever tasted).

But most of all, it's why I decided to reveal my secret recipes—the special ones, the cherished ones, the ones I have spent a lifetime perfecting and, until now, saved for family, special times, and special friends.

Like the time back in 1972 when I gave Laura Nyro one of my top secret recipes as a wedding gift. This recipe was for potato salad, and Laura had been begging me for it for almost a year, ever since the day she came to Philly to hang out with me for the day and I served it, along with some serious barbecue chicken, for lunch.

"Oooooh, Pat," Laura shrieked, when she tasted it. "I am not leaving here until you give me this recipe. I have *never* had any potato salad like this."

"Well, Girlfriend, I guess you better call the moving van because, if you think you're getting my potato salad recipe, I have three words for you: Ain't no way."

"Come on, Pat," she persisted. "Why not?"

"For one thing, it's a family secret," I told her. "And for another, you're used to White people's potato salad; this recipe is for Sisters."

Of course, to me Laura *was* a sister. In both senses of the word. We were as close as family and, the first time I heard her play the piano and sing, I told her I was going to make her an honorary Sister. "Honey," I said, "you are a Black woman in a White girl's body."

If you've ever listened to Laura's music, you know exactly what I mean. It is so

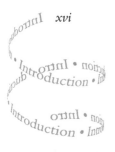

soulful. And, whenever we were together, that's what Laura always wanted to sing—soul music.

Right after I got married, Laura used to come and stay with Armstead and me in our tiny little one-bedroom apartment on Johnson Street. Now, you could have fit my apartment into hers twenty times and still had room left over but, for some reason, Laura loved that place. She said it had a certain peacefulness about it, a spiritual vibe that she loved.

Sometimes, she'd come and stay for weeks at a time, and we'd spend all day in the kitchen doing what we loved best: singing, harmonizing, and trying out new recipes. One day, after we'd cooked some fried chicken that would put the Colonel's to shame, Laura and I decided we were going to open up a restaurant. Fortunately, before we sank any money into the idea, we came to our senses. "Between the two of us," Laura said, polishing off a wing, "we'd eat all the profits."

Laura loved soul food as much as she loved soul music. Which is why when she called to tell me she was getting married, I knew what I had to do. And I did it without a moment's hesitation. But first, I swore her to secrecy. After she'd taken an oath of silence, I took her through my potato salad recipe—ingredient by ingredient, step by step.

"My money is funny right now," I explained, "so this will have to be my wedding gift to you and David. You're the only person outside the family I've shared it with. You know I love you like a sister and I always will."

By the time we hung up the phone, I don't know who was crying hardest, Laura or me. Almost two years later, when my son Zuri was born and I went into a serious postpartum depression, it was Laura who saved my sanity. Just as she had threatened to do that day at the kitchen table, she moved in with me. But not to get my potato salad recipe; to care for Zuri and me until I was strong enough to care for us both. The day Laura left, I told her even if I gave her every single one of my recipes I would never be able to repay her.

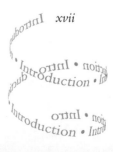

"Don't worry about it, Pat," she said, kissing me on the cheek and waving good-bye. "That's what friends are for."

Laura died not long ago, but my memories of her and our special times together in my kitchen on Johnson Street will live in my heart forever.

What's amazing to me, though I guess it shouldn't be, is how many of my happiest memories have occurred in the kitchen. Starting with that tiny little apartment on Johnson Street, wherever I've lived, the kitchen has always been the center and soul of my home, the place where everybody congregates—I don't care how many other rooms there are in the house.

It doesn't matter how crowded the kitchen gets, either. Folks will just keep squeezing inside until it's standing room only. For the longest time, I can't tell you how much that annoyed me. Many a day just getting from the stove to the table without spilling a pot of hot greens or hitting somebody upside the head with it was a real test of skill, patience, and endurance.

For the longest time, the way people jammed themselves into my kitchen like French fries when I was trying to get dinner on the table drove me absolutely crazy. It used to make me so mad I could scream, until Armstead made me see why the kitchen is everyone's favorite spot in the house.

"People gather in the kitchen," he said, "not just to put food in their mouth but to put joy in their spirit. To feed their hunger for connection as well as refection."

I'll never forget the day Armstead told me that. I was in no mood for any of his sociological analysis. It was ninety degrees outside, the air-conditioning had gone on the fritz, and I was cooking dinner for twenty people, fifteen of whom were sitting in my kitchen. "If you don't get all these people out of my kitchen by the time I count to twenty," I told Armstead, "they're going to be wearing my macaroni and cheese instead of eating it."

That night, after my dinner guests departed and the air-conditioning repairman arrived, I thought about what Armstead had said. And the more I thought

about it, the more I knew he was right about "the call of the kitchen." People gather in the kitchen to be nurtured as well as nourished. Since the day I grasped that truth, I haven't put a single soul out of my kitchen. I did, however, enlarge it to three times its original size!

Now, every time I look around my new kitchen, I feel so blessed that my friends and family want to be there. The truth is, I need them in my kitchen as much as, if not more than, they need to be there. It's just like the award-winning playwright/novelist/poet Ntozake Shange says in her book *If I Can Cook/You Know God Can:* "When my house starts to smell like no one's cookin' in it, no one's sighed deeply after a dish of blueberry cobbler or sweet potato puffs, I find myself questioning my own value, what I value, what is a well-lived life."

I know what Sister Ntozake means. If I didn't cook, I'd probably be crazy. Depending on when you ask Armstead, he might tell you I am. Seriously, though, if I didn't cook, I don't know what I'd do. Like singing, cooking has always been my therapy, the thing that kept me sane whenever life got crazy. Usually, when people are feeling stressed out they want a pill, but honey, give me a pot. For me, time in the kitchen is like time on the couch. Better, since I don't have to pay somebody 100 bucks an hour to be there.

I can't explain it, but there is just something about the slicing, the stirring, the baking, the brewing that stills my soul; something about the rhythm of mixing the ingredients that calms me, comforts me, cools me completely out. Armstead says I am the only person in the world who has found her panacea in a pan.

Cooking has had that effect on me since I was little girl. As a kid, I fantasized about cooking almost as much as I fantasized about singing. I would make believe I was a celebrated singer *and* a celebrated chef. On those days when the bribes Chubby and Naomi offered me to get me to go outside didn't work and they threatened to beat my behind unless I got out of the kitchen, I would head straight for my hideout: the shed in our backyard. Of course, in my mind it wasn't a shed. Depending on what day it was, in my mind, it was either a concert

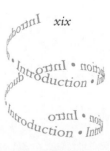

hall or world-famous restaurant. And not just any concert hall—Harlem's world-famous Apollo Theater. And not just any restaurant—*my* world-famous restaurant: Patsy Holte's House of Fabulous Foods.

And fabulous it was, at least in my imagination. I would make believe all my favorite singers came there to eat. In my daydreams, all the divas of the day—Gloria Lynne, Dakota Staton, Sarah Vaughn—came to my restaurant to dine. It was *the* place to go, *the* place to eat, *the* place to see and be seen.

While the other kids played house, I played restaurant. I'd chat with my favorite singers, then I'd "cook" them a meal fit for the stars they were. A bucket was my sink, a Sterno can was my stove, and my hairbrush served double duty as my microphone or whatever utensil I needed to stir, slice, or serve my feast. I would spend hours in that shed making believe I was talking with my idols about their music and my meals.

After "dinner," I would make believe someone would ask me to sing.

"Pick anything you want, Patsy," I imagined Gloria or Dakota saying. "We just want to hear you sing something."

Of course, I never said yes the first time they asked me. Even at that young age, I guess there was a little diva in me who wanted to be coaxed.

"Come on, Patsy," I imagined them insisting. "Just one song."

How could I refuse? They weren't just my idols, they were my best customers! And so, as fast as you can say "just my imagination running away with me," Patsy the world-famous chef would become Patsy the world-famous singer. Using my hairbrush as my mike, I would sing my heart out. Who would have guessed that, forty years later, I'd still be cooking and singing? The only difference is now my mike and my stove are real.

So are the stars I've cooked for: Elton John, Gladys Knight, Toni Braxton, and Oprah Winfrey, to name a few. Back in the eighties, I cooked a feast for the Rolling Stones. They had come to Philly to give a concert at RFK Stadium, and I had just come off the road myself. I was deep down into a serious sleep when the phone woke me up.

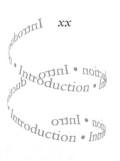

"Patti," the voice on the other end said. "How about cooking us one of your fabulous meals?"

I have to be dreaming, I thought. There is no way this could be who I think it is.

"Mick Jagger," I said. "Is that you?"

"It's me," he answered.

I was too through. "No, you didn't have the nerve to wake me up in the middle of the night to ask me to cook you some food," I said.

But I didn't mind. Mick and I went way back. All the way to the mid sixties when Sarah Dash, Nona Hendryx, and I were touring the country as Patti LaBelle and the Bluebells and we were the Stones' opening act. Mick, Keith, and the guys were always good to us, and I will never forget how angry Mick got when Jim Crow laws forced us to stay in different hotels when we were performing in the South.

As soon as I hung up, I started making my grocery list. Armstead was not happy when I asked him to go to the market with a list as long as his arm. And he was *really* mad when he saw the bill.

I wish you could have seen all the food I cooked for Mick and the guys: platters of pasta, baskets of bread, kettles of greens, pans of shrimp, chicken, turkey, and fish. I didn't know what they were into—meat, fish, pasta, salads—so I just fixed everything. I cooked so much food that Mick had to send a van over to my house to pick it all up.

While Armstead wasn't happy, I was in heaven. I'd never tell Mick, of course, but I had as much fun cooking that food for the Stones as they had eating it. That sense of wonder I felt as a kid "cooking" in our backyard shed has never left me. If anything, over the years, my passion for cooking has only gotten stronger.

I know people think I'm kidding when I tell them I take my pans out on tour with me, but I am as serious as a heart attack. Not only do I take them with me, they're the first thing I pack. If you open my suitcase, you'll find three or four pans right beside my designer gowns. They're like my American Express card—I don't leave home without them.

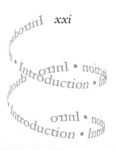

That's because I cook on tour as much as I do at home; I just do it for different reasons. For one thing, I cannot stand hotel food—it's too bland, too tasteless, too much money. But there's another reason I cook so much when I'm out on tour, a reason that's much more important to me than my problem with hotel food. Singing for a live audience is such a spiritual experience for me, cooking is the only way I can come down from the high I'm on after I give a concert. I've tried everything—bubble baths, massages, saunas—but nothing relaxes me the way cooking does. Nothing.

When I finish a show, I like to come back to the hotel, put on my pajamas, and spread out my goodies: my seasonings, my pans, all the fabulous food finds I've discovered in whatever city I'm in for the night. Many a night I'll cook until the wee hours of the morning. When I'm feeling really good, I'll prepare enough food for the whole band, and the guys will drop by my room and pick up a plate to go.

If I have a really strong craving for something, or if I don't have the ingredients I want, I'll go grocery shopping after a show. Sometimes, if the show runs long and I don't want to go back to the hotel and change my clothes, I will go grocery shopping in my gown. It drives my bodyguard crazy. "Relax," I always tell him. "Nobody is going to bother me in the vegetable aisle."

People have the funniest reactions when they see me in the grocery store. Some stare, some scream, some run up and down the aisles. A lot of people just don't believe it's me. "Patti, that's not really you, is it?" I've been asked more times than I can count.

Sometimes, when I'm really in a hurry, I'm tempted to pretend I'm a Patti impersonator. But I don't; at least I haven't yet. I always tell the truth. "Yeah, Sugar, it's me. But don't tell anybody; I just want to get my onions and tomatoes and get out of here."

Once, I gave a mini concert in the seasoning aisle. Some of my die-hard fans, fans from way back in the sixties, spotted me searching for some sea salt. The

next thing I knew, they were telling me about all the shows they'd come to over the years. We're talking *dozens*. They remembered concerts *I* had forgotten. "You all have been to almost as many shows as I have," I told them.

Of course, that they would come to see me all those times just touched my heart. So, when they asked me if I would please sing a little something, what could I do? My bodyguard didn't speak to me the whole way home.

I love to grocery shop. It takes me back to the days when Chubby used to take me with her to the Italian market to buy our food for the week. Every Saturday morning, the two of us would head over to Henry Colt's Poultry Market down on Ninth and Washington Avenue. Chubby refused to buy her chickens anywhere else. She said Henry had the freshest chickens in town.

For meats, we went over to Phil's Market on 84th Street. Phil's meats were as fresh as Henry's chickens. When you cut into a piece of Phil's beef, I swear it would moo. Chubby never went home without an armful of bags. "Child," she used to say, "we've got to have plenty of food in the house. You never know who's coming over."

I'm the same way today. At home, I keep two freezers full of food. Like Chubby said, you just never know when folks are going to drop by. Besides, I might wake up at two in the morning and feel like cooking. And since I can't drive (I haven't been behind the wheel of a car since the day Armstead tried to teach me to drive and I crashed his brand-new Thunderbird into a tree), I'd have to wake him up and ask him to take me grocery shopping. And you can guess how that would go over. Like Pat Boone at the New Orleans jazz fest.

Now if I'm out on the road that's a different story. If I'm out on the road, odds are better than fifty-fifty that I can talk my traveling companion/hairdresser/best friend, Norma, into going shopping with me no matter what time it is. So, if you hear I'm in town, look for me at a grocery store near you.

I have so many more stories—and recipes—to share and they're all in this book: setting off the fire alarms in Caesar's Palace while cooking liver and

onions for Arsenio Hall, sending Armstead out for hard-shell crabs on our wedding night, spilling a pot of boiling grease on my neck (I still carry the scars) trying to fish out a piece of fatback, to name a few.

Some stories—like the flying biscuits—are hard to believe. Some stories—like the kindness of Laura Nyro—are hard to forget. But the recipes that go with them are all precious to me. And now they're my gift to you.

Before you head for the kitchen, though, we need to talk about the recipes. They're all fly-you-to-the-moon good. But some, like my five-cheese Over-the-Rainbow Macaroni and Cheese, are not for everyday eating. You have to remember, back when I started cooking, we thought fat was something God put in food to make it taste good. Of course, now we know better. Now we know that dishes high in calories and fat should be special treats, not everyday indulgences. And since I learned I was a diabetic, I know that more than most.

Now get your apron, Sugar, and let's do some cooking Patti-style.

Sensational Salads, Soups, and Sandwiches

Sunday Salad with Versatile Vinaigrette

When you have a crowd coming for a Sunday dinner and you want a big green salad, you can't do better than this one, packed with everything a salad should have in it. The vinaigrette will probably become your "house dressing," as it has mine.

Makes **8 to 10** servings

VERSATILE VINAIGRETTE

¼ cup red wine vinegar
2 tablespoons balsamic vinegar
1 garlic clove, minced
¾ cup olive oil
Salt and freshly ground black pepper

16 cups assorted salad greens, preferably equal
    amounts of spinach, curly endive, arugula, and
    iceberg lettuce
2 large ripe tomatoes, chopped
1 medium cucumber, peeled and sliced
1 medium onion, thinly sliced
One 2.25-ounce can sliced ripe olives, drained
2 tablespoons chopped fresh oregano
2 tablespoons chopped fresh cilantro
2 tablespoons capers, drained
2 garlic cloves, minced

To make the vinaigrette: Combine the wine vinegar, balsamic vinegar, garlic, and oil in a glass jar. Season with salt and pepper to taste. Close the jar tightly and shake well until the dressing is thick and emulsified. (Or, in a medium bowl, whisk the wine vinegar, balsamic vinegar, garlic, salt, and pepper. Gradually whisk in the oil.) Use immediately, or refrigerate, covered, for up to 3 days. Shake well before serving.

In a large bowl, toss the salad greens, tomatoes, cucumber, onion, olives, oregano, cilantro, capers, and garlic. Drizzle with the vinaigrette and toss again. Serve immediately.

Naomi's Creamy Coleslaw

Growing up in Philly, I can't remember when my mother's best friend, Naomi, didn't live with us. Naomi Thompson was like a second mother to me, and she loved me like I was her own. Like my daddy, Naomi believed cleanliness was next to godliness. That applied to kids as well as kitchens. Until I got too big to fit into it, Naomi used to bathe me in the kitchen sink. "Child," she would say shaking her head, "you've got the rustiest behind I've ever seen."

Like Chubby, Naomi could really get down in the kitchen. Still can. Like most great cooks I know, Naomi cooks everything from scratch and never measures an ingredient. Come to think of it, in all the years I have known her, I have never once seen Naomi open a cookbook, although she sure could write one.

Whenever I wanted to learn how to make one of her dishes, Naomi would patiently walk me through the right way to prepare it; add a bit of this but never that, shake but never stir, cook on high heat at first, then simmer very slowly.

Around the neighborhood, Naomi's recipes were much in demand—especially her coleslaw. Once you ate it, you didn't want anybody else's. Try it and you'll see why.

Salads, Soups, and Sandwiches

1 medium head green cabbage
   (2½ pounds)
1 large carrot, shredded
½ cup finely chopped onion
1 cup mayonnaise
2 tablespoons white vinegar
1 teaspoon sugar
Salt and crushed red pepper flakes

Cut the cabbage into quarters. Cut off and discard the hard core from each wedge. Using a large knife, finely shred the cabbage. (The cabbage can also be sliced with a food processor fitted with the slicing blade. Do not use the shredding blade.)

   In a large bowl, combine the cabbage, carrot, and onion. In a small bowl, stir the mayonnaise, vinegar, and sugar together until well combined. Pour the dressing over the slaw and mix well. Season with salt and red pepper flakes to taste. Cover and refrigerate until well chilled, at least 4 hours or overnight. Serve chilled.

Patti's Pointers: Be sure and taste the salad before you serve it. If it has been refrigerated for a while, it sometimes needs more salt and pepper and maybe a splash of vinegar.

Patti's Potato Salad

I can laugh about it now. But, three years ago, my potato salad almost had me in tears in front of fifteen million people on national television. For years, Oprah Winfrey had been hearing through the grapevine that I made potato salad like nobody else.

"Patti, girl," she said to me one day. "If one more person tells me about your potato salad before I get to taste it, I am not going to be happy. Will you make me some?"

Oprah and me laughing at the first batch of Patti's Potato Salad.

"I'll make you my potato salad and anything else you want," I told Oprah. And I meant it. She is one of the most special people in the world to me.

Well, you know what they say about the best laid plans. Between our two schedules, Oprah and I were never in the same city long enough for me to even boil the potatoes. Which is why, in the fall of '96, when I was booked to appear on her show, I called Oprah and told her I would make my potato salad for her whole audience.

I'll spare you the gory details, but, suffice it to say, because of scheduling conflicts, I couldn't get to Chicago in time to grocery shop, make the potato salad, and get over to Harpo Studios on time for the show. So I did the only thing I could: I gave my recipe to a professional caterer with detailed instructions on how to prepare it.

When I arrived at Oprah's studio, something told me I should ask to taste the potato salad. And am I ever glad I did! You should have seen that soupy mess they were trying to pass off as Patti's Potato Salad. And it tasted even worse than it looked!

"There is no way I'm claiming this," I told Armstead, as I heard Oprah introducing me. "I'll just explain to the audience what happened after the show."

And that's exactly what I did. But poor Oprah. I didn't get a chance to warn her about the potato salad before we went on the air. As she was giving out the recipe, I watched in horror as Oprah helped herself to a nice big spoonful. I know she wanted to choke but, to Oprah's credit, she just kept smiling and chewing that nasty potato salad as if it was the best thing in the world. The next thing I knew we were going to commercial.

"Somebody get me a glass of water," Oprah said when the cameras stopped rolling. Then she turned to me. "You know I always tell my audience the truth," she said, "and the truth is this potato salad needs help."

"The caterers messed it up; I'll explain everything after the show," I promised.

Oprah and I still laugh about that day. "Girl, you should have seen yourself chewing those hard-as-rocks potatoes, trying to smile and act like nothing was wrong."

Before I left Chicago, I tried to make it up to Oprah. I sent her a bowl of the *real* Patti's Potato Salad big enough to feed her whole staff.

Eat and enjoy!

3 pounds red-skinned potatoes
   (20 potatoes), well scrubbed
6 large eggs, hard-cooked
   (see Note)
1 medium red onion, finely chopped
1 medium green bell pepper, seeded and finely
   chopped
2 medium celery ribs, finely chopped
2 teaspoons celery seed
⅔ cup mayonnaise
2 tablespoons yellow mustard
3 tablespoons sweet pickle relish
Salt and freshly ground black pepper
Paprika

Place the potatoes in a large pot and add enough salted water to cover by 1 inch. Bring to a boil over high heat. Reduce the heat to medium-low and simmer until tender, but not mushy, about 20 minutes. Be sure they are cooked! Pour out most of the water and place the pot in the sink. Run cold water over the potatoes for about 2 minutes, or until cool enough to handle. Drain well.

Peel the potatoes and cut them into ½-inch cubes. Place in a large bowl. Chop 4 hard-cooked eggs and add to the potatoes, along with the red onion, green pepper, and celery. Sprinkle with the celery seed. Gradually stir in the mayonnaise, mustard, and relish (wear rubber or plastic gloves and use your hands, if you wish), being careful not to smash the potatoes. Season with salt and pepper to taste.

Transfer to a large serving bowl. Slice the 2 remaining hard-cooked eggs. Arrange the slices on top of the salad and sprinkle with paprika. Serve immediately, or cool, cover tightly with plastic wrap, and refrigerate until chilled, at least 2 hours.

Note: *I know that most people actually boil their eggs to hard-cook them, but if you overdo it, you can get that thin green line around the yolk that everyone just hates. Here's the foolproof professional way to hard-cook eggs that cuts down on the actual boiling time to avoid overcooking. Place the eggs in a saucepan just large enough to hold them in one layer. Fill with enough cold water to cover by 1 inch. Bring to a gentle boil over high heat. Cook for 30 seconds. Remove from the stove and cover tightly. Let stand for 15 minutes. Pour out most of the water and place the pan in the sink. Let cold water run over the eggs for about 3 minutes. Crack and peel the eggs while still warm.*

Patti's Pointers: I use red-skinned potatoes because the slices retain their shape when the salad is tossed—russets and Idaho potatoes will crumble. Remember: Always choose smooth, firm potatoes that have no bruises. Wash the potatoes just when you are ready to use them. Don't store the potatoes in the refrigerator because they will turn dark when you cook them. Be sure to cut off any greenish discoloration because it will have a bitter taste. For a potato salad with kick, I sometimes spice this salad up with 2 seeded and minced jalapeño peppers.

Company's-Coming Chicken Salad

This is wonderful for lunch as a salad on greens, and it's also the best sandwich filling around. It can also be made with leftover chicken or store-bought roasted chicken. 🎼

4 chicken breast halves, with skin and bones (about
    2¾ pounds)
1 small yellow onion, sliced
1 teaspoon salt, plus more to taste
¼ teaspoon freshly ground black pepper, plus more
    to taste
2 medium celery ribs, cut into
    ¼-inch dice
1 small red onion, finely chopped
½ medium green bell pepper, seeded and cut into
    ¼-inch dice (½ cup)
1 garlic clove, minced
3 hard-cooked eggs, peeled and chopped (see Note,
    page 9)
⅓ cup sweet pickle relish
1 cup mayonnaise
Crushed red pepper flakes
Green or Boston lettuce leaves
Paprika

Place the chicken and sliced onion in a large saucepan and add enough cold water to cover. Add 1 teaspoon salt and ¼ teaspoon pepper. Cover and bring to a boil over medium-high heat. Reduce the heat to medium-low. Simmer just until the chicken shows no sign of pink when pierced in the thickest part, about 20 minutes. Remove from the heat and let cool in the liquid. Remove and discard the skin and bones, and cut the meat into ¾-inch pieces. Cool completely.

In a large bowl, combine the chicken, celery, red onion, green pepper, garlic, eggs, and relish. Gently stir in the mayonnaise, seasoning with the red pepper flakes and additional salt and pepper to taste. Cover and refrigerate until chilled, about 1 hour.

Place the lettuce leaves on individual salad plates. Spoon the chicken salad on the lettuce leaves, sprinkle with paprika, and serve.

Classic Crabmeat Salad in Tomato Cups

Makes 4 servings

1 pound fresh crabmeat, preferably backfin, picked
    over to remove cartilage
⅔ cup mayonnaise
⅓ cup finely chopped onion
⅓ cup finely chopped celery
1 hard-cooked egg, finely chopped (see Note,
    page 9)
Salt and freshly ground black pepper
2 large ripe tomatoes
1 small head green leaf lettuce,
    separated into leaves, well rinsed and dried
Paprika
Lemon wedges

In a medium bowl, mix the crabmeat, mayonnaise, onion, celery, and hard-cooked egg. Season with salt and pepper to taste. Cover and refrigerate until well chilled, about 2 hours.

Cut each tomato in half horizontally. Using a dessertspoon, scoop out and discard the inside of each tomato half to leave a shell. Season the inside of each tomato with salt and pepper. Fill each shell with the chilled crabmeat salad and place on a lettuce leaf. Sprinkle with paprika and serve with lemon wedges.

Patti's Pointers: Go to a good fish store to buy fresh, not canned or pasteurized, crabmeat. It usually comes in 1-pound containers. This just isn't worth making with so-so crab.

Geechee Geechee Ya Ya Gumbo

There's no use making a small pot of gumbo. You'll only wish you made more, anyway. One of the secrets to a great (not just a really good) gumbo is lots of ingredients. When I make my gumbo, I cram it full of good things—sausage, chicken, shrimp, oysters, and crabmeat. But, if you want to leave out the oysters and crabmeat, that's fine, too. The gumbo will still be fab-u-lous.

Filé powder, sometimes called filé gumbo, is ground sassafras leaves, which acts more as a thickener than a seasoning. Filé shouldn't be simmered, or it gives the gumbo a stringy, gummy consistency. This soup is thick enough for most people without the filé, but for some cooks, without filé, it's not gumbo. Here's a good rule of thumb: If you know you are going to have leftover gumbo that will be reheated, don't use the filé, or only add it to the gumbo *just before serving.* Reheated, filé-seasoned gumbo will get a pretty nasty texture. If you live in the South, filé is pretty easy to find. Otherwise, look for it in the spice or fish departments of well-stocked supermarkets or specialty food stores.

See what I mean about my family members crowding in the kitchen until it's standing room only? Uncle Jack; my son Zuri; my nieces Stephanie, Fahja, and beautiful baby Mikaela hang out in their favorite room in the house as they wait for a pot of my gumbo to get done.

½ cup plus 2 tablespoons
   vegetable oil

1 pound andouille, smoked hot links, or kielbasa sausage, cut
   into ½-inch pieces

2 large onions, chopped

2 medium green bell peppers, seeded and chopped

4 medium celery ribs, chopped

4 garlic cloves, minced

½ cup all-purpose flour

2½ cups water

1 pound fresh okra, trimmed,
   cut into ¼-inch-thick rounds

One 28-ounce can crushed tomatoes

3½ cups chicken broth

2 teaspoons dried thyme leaves

1 teaspoon crushed red pepper flakes

3 bay leaves

1 teaspoon salt, plus more to taste

1 teaspoon freshly ground black pepper, plus more to taste

1 pound boneless, skinless
   chicken breast, cut into
   bite-sized cubes

2 cups fresh or thawed frozen
   corn kernels (see Note, page 18)

1 pound crabmeat, picked over
   to remove cartilage

1 pound medium shrimp,
   peeled and deveined (leave the tail segment
   attached, if desired)

2 cups shucked oysters (about 18 oysters)

4 teaspoons filé (gumbo) powder, optional

A double recipe of Perfectly Steamed Rice (page 135)

In a large pot, heat 2 tablespoons of the oil over medium heat. Add the sausage, onions, bell peppers, celery, and garlic. Cook, stirring occasionally, until the vegetables are tender, about 10 minutes. Using a slotted spoon, transfer to a bowl.

Add the remaining $^1/_2$ cup of oil to the pot. Gradually stir in the flour and reduce the heat to medium-low. Cook, stirring almost constantly, until the mixture turns light brown, about 5 minutes. The mixture will smell toasty, but don't let it burn!

Gradually stir in the water. Stir in the reserved vegetables and sausage, okra, tomatoes, broth, thyme, red pepper flakes, bay leaves, 1 teaspoon salt, and 1 teaspoon black pepper. Bring to a boil over high heat. Reduce the heat to medium-low and cook, uncovered, for 1 hour. Add the chicken and corn and cook for 20 minutes. Add the crabmeat, shrimp, and oysters, and cook until the shrimp are pink and firm, about 3 minutes. Remove from the heat. Stir in the filé powder, if desired, and let stand for 5 minutes. Season with additional salt and pepper. Remove the bay leaves.

To serve, spoon the rice into individual soup bowls. Ladle the gumbo over the rice. Serve hot.

Budd's Back-to-Life Soup

I created this recipe for one of my oldest and dearest friends—my musical director of almost thirty years, James "Budd" Ellison. For much of his life, Budd was a vegetarian. But, when a recent medical examination revealed he had cancer, doctors told Budd he had to start eating chicken and red meat again.

"I'm going to make you wonder why you ever gave up either one," I told Budd the night he told me about the diagnosis. "We're going to fight this thing together."

My friend, the super-talented Budd Ellison, and his beautiful bride, Barbara.

And that's just what we're doing. Whenever we're out on tour, I try to cook Budd something special, something full of vitamins and protein that I know he'll love. I created this soup for him the first night he came back out on the road with me after going through his treatments.

To tell you the truth, I wasn't sure he would like it. For one thing, Budd hadn't eaten chicken in twenty-five years. For another, like me, Budd's a really picky eater. Hours after I had sent the soup to Budd's room, I hadn't heard a word from him. I assumed he hated it and he hadn't called because he wanted to spare my feelings.

It was after midnight when I heard a knock at my door.

"Hey, Pat," Budd said, handing me the empty pot. "Any more soup left?"

I was so happy I wanted to cry. "No, Sugar," I said, fighting back tears. "But come on in. I'll make you a fresh pot."

When you serve Budd's soup, finish your bowl the way he'd want you to. Swab it clean with some nice crusty bread! 🎼

Makes 8 to 10 servings

One 3½-pound chicken
Salt and freshly ground black pepper
2 medium onions, chopped
1 medium leek, white part with 2 inches of light
   green top, chopped and well rinsed
8 ounces green beans, trimmed,
   cut into 1-inch lengths
2 cups fresh or frozen corn kernels (see Note, page 18)
3 medium carrots, chopped
One 15-ounce can diced tomatoes, with juice
1 small green bell pepper, seeded and chopped
2 garlic cloves, chopped

Rinse the chicken under cold running water. Season well, inside and out, with salt and pepper. Place in a soup pot and add enough lightly salted cold water to barely cover. Bring to a boil over high heat. Skim off any foam that rises to the surface. Reduce heat to medium-low and cover. Simmer until the meat falls off the bone, about 1½ hours. Remove the chicken from the broth. Remove and discard the skin and bones. Chop the meat and set aside.

Add the onions, leek, green beans, corn, carrots, tomatoes, bell pepper, and garlic to the broth. Simmer until the vegetables are tender, about 30 minutes. Return the meat to the broth. Skim any fat from the surface. Season with salt and pepper. Serve hot.

Patti's Pointers: This wonderful chicken soup is full of vegetable flavor. Just as it contains Budd's favorite veggies, you can use your favorites, too. Add zucchini or peas or celery, if you wish.

Smoky Corn and Turkey Chowder

Makes **6 to 8** servings

5 cups chicken broth
One 1½-pound smoked turkey wing
3 cups fresh corn, cut from the cob (see Note), or
    thawed frozen corn
1 medium onion, chopped
1 medium carrot, cut into ½-inch dice
1 medium celery rib, cut into ½-inch dice
1 large russet or Idaho potato, peeled and cut into
    ½-inch dice
¾ cup heavy cream
Seasoned salt and freshly ground black pepper
Chopped fresh parsley

In a Dutch oven, combine the chicken broth, turkey wing, corn kernels, onion, carrot, celery, and potato. Bring to a simmer over medium heat, stirring often. Reduce the heat to low and simmer until the vegetables are tender, about 20 minutes.

Remove the turkey wing from the chowder. Discard the skin and bones. Chop the meat. Return the meat to the pot.

Add the cream and heat through, but do not boil. Season with salt and pepper. Serve hot, sprinkling each serving with parsley.

Note: *To cut corn from the cob, shuck the corn and remove the silk. Rinse under cold water. Using a sharp knife, slice the kernels off each cob into a large bowl. Using the knife, scrape any remaining corn and the corn milk from each cob into the bowl. You usually get about ½ cup kernels from a medium-sized ear. Large ears will yield ¾ to 1 cup.*

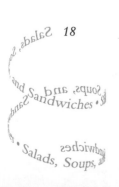

Jackie's Fried Egg Sandwich

I have come to terms with it now. But it took me years to forgive myself. Years of remorse. Years of regret. Years of really serious suffering. There were times when I thought I would never—not ever—make peace with it. And while I have forgiven myself for what happened, I haven't forgotten. The truth is, I never want to. The lesson is too important.

Many of you know the story; I've told it hundreds, maybe thousands, of times—in my autobiography, in my concerts, in interview after interview. But its lesson is so important, so life-changing, that it bears heeding and repeating.

It's the story of how I refused my baby sister's last wish. Not refused, exactly. Put her off with promises —promises that I never got to keep. Jackie was in the hospital receiving treatments for brain cancer, and I had been running back and forth to see her for days. I was home resting when she called me. I couldn't have been there more than a few hours, and I almost didn't answer the phone. But I did. And that phone call would change my life forever.

I listened in silence as Jackie told me what she wanted: an egg sandwich. But not any egg sandwich. *My* egg sandwich. The way I had been making it for her since she was just a little kid. You see, the chemotherapy treatments had made Jackie so sick she didn't want any of the hospital food. That she wanted

My baby sister, Jackie, and my dad, Henry Holte, were as close as two peas in a pod.

food at all—mine or anybody else's—was a small miracle. She hadn't had an appetite since she'd been admitted to the hospital and, truth be told, it was the first time in days that I'd heard Jackie say she was hungry. But not for anyone's cooking. Just mine. She said my egg sandwich was the only thing she had a taste for. It was the only thing she thought she could keep down.

"Please, Patsy," Jackie said. "I'm hungry for one of your egg sandwiches. Will you make it for me?"

The thought of turning around and going back to the hospital made me wince. It was selfish, I know, but I was bone tired and, at that moment, I just didn't think I could handle it. And so I took the coward's way out. I stalled. "I'm tired," I told her. "I'll make it later."

As many people know, later never came. And I never got to fulfill my sister's last wish. After that phone call, Jackie got worse. At the end, she was on a respirator and in and out of consciousness. And before I could keep my promise, she died.

You want to know the cruelest irony of all? The night before she passed, I made a promise to myself: that I would be less selfish, more giving, with Jackie. I promised myself I would be a better sister to her, the kind of sister she had always wanted, the kind of sister she deserved. The kind of sister she had always been to me.

That night I vowed, from that moment on, I would give Jackie the only thing she ever really wanted from me—my time and my attention—and stop trying to substitute money and gifts for either one.

I was about to leave for the hospital when the phone rang. I know it wasn't rational, but I thought it was Jackie calling to say, "I'm feeling better now, Patsy, so don't you even think about showing up without my egg sandwich." But it wasn't Jackie. It was Aunt Hattie Mae. She was calling from Jackie's room, and I could tell by her voice that something was terribly wrong. I didn't let her say more than my name before I cut her off.

"No. Don't tell me, Aunt Hattie Mae."

Her next words left me numb. "It's true, Baby. Jackie's gone. But she didn't suffer. She just slept away."

In the ten years that have passed since Jackie's death, I have tried to keep the lesson of that day—Armstead and I call it the egg sandwich lesson—in front of me. I have tried not only to spread its message, but to live it. As I tell anyone who will listen: *The smallest deed is greater than the grandest intention.* It really is. Believe me, I know. Because of Jackie and the egg sandwich, I'm a much better person. Now, I say what I feel when I'm feeling it. I do what I have to do when I'm supposed to do it. I go where I need to be when I need to be there. Most important of all, nobody I love—not one single person—will ever leave this world again without hearing from me how much they mean to me. And I have Jackie to thank for that precious gift.

This recipe is for her. But I hope what it symbolizes will be a reminder to us all.

Makes 1 wonderful sandwich

2 tablespoons olive oil
2 tablespoons butter
2 slices white sandwich bread
2 large eggs
Salt and freshly ground black pepper

In a medium nonstick skillet, heat the oil over medium heat until hot and shimmering, but not smoking. In a large skillet, melt the butter over medium heat.

Place the bread in the large skillet and cook on one side only until the underside is golden brown, about 3½ minutes.

Meanwhile, crack the eggs into the skillet. Season with a sprinkle each of salt and pepper. Cook until the whites are just set and turning golden around edges, about 2 minutes. Using a spatula, pierce the yolks so they run over the whites. Cook just until the yolks are barely set, but not hard, about 1 more minute.

Transfer the bread to a plate, toasted sides down. Place the eggs on one slice, and top with the other slice, toasted side out. Serve immediately.

Patti's Pointers: Fry the egg and the bread in tandem in two separate skillets, timing them so they're done about the same time. Everyone has a different idea on when a fried egg is done—over, up, runny, hard. Cook this the way you like, but keep in mind that when you put the eggs between two hot slices of bread, they will cook some more. This is the way Jackie liked hers.

The Great Grilled Cheese Sandwich

When I make a cheese sandwich, I make a *cheese sandwich*—gooey and outrageous. If you aren't feeling all that indulgent, you can cut back to two slices of cheese. Make this in a nonstick skillet—the cheese will ooze out of the sandwich into the pan and cook until toasty and chewy and altogether incredible. If you use a regular skillet, the cheese will just burn.

Makes 1 outrageous serving

4 slices American cheese
2 slices potato bread
2 slices tomato
Dried oregano
Crushed red pepper flakes
2 tablespoons butter

Stack the cheese on 1 slice of the bread. Microwave on High (100%) until softened and beginning to melt, 30 to 45 seconds. Top with the tomato, season with the oregano and red pepper flakes, and cover with the second slice of bread.

   In a large nonstick skillet, melt the butter over medium-high heat. Add the sandwich and top with a plate to weight the sandwich down. Cook until the underside is golden, about 2 minutes. Don't worry about the cheese coming out of the sandwich—it will cook to a crusty brown consistency by the time the sandwich is finished. Turn the sandwich, top with the plate, and cook until the other side is golden, about 2 more minutes. Serve immediately.

Simple, Simply Delicious Smoked Turkey Sandwich

I love fried ham sandwiches the way some people love chocolate. That is to say beyond all logic and reason. Sometimes, I crave a fried ham sandwich the way a pregnant woman craves pickles and ice cream. And, like a tall glass of water when you're really, really thirsty, nothing else can satisfy that craving.

Or so I thought until recently when a fried smoked turkey sandwich changed my mind. At the time, I was desperate. I was having a serious gotta-have-me-a-fried-ham-sandwich attack, but I knew I shouldn't. I had recently learned I was diabetic, and my doctors made it clear the only way I could manage this disease was to take my medication and change my eating habits. Doing one without the other, they said, wasn't going to cut it. I had to take my pills and cut back on all kinds of food I loved—including pork.

And so, cooking my smoked turkey sandwich was a desperation move. At best, I thought it might take the edge off my fried ham craving, but I didn't expect it to really satisfy it.

To my amazement, that fried smoked turkey sandwich was fantastic! Every bit as good as my beloved fried ham sandwich. But don't take my word for it . . . see for yourself.

Makes 4 sandwiches

1 tablespoon vegetable oil
1 pound smoked turkey breast, sliced ⅛ inch thick
8 slices white sandwich bread
4 tablespoons mayonnaise
1 ripe large tomato, thinly sliced
4 large lettuce leaves

Pour the oil into a large nonstick skillet, tilt the pan to coat the bottom with the oil, and place over medium heat. In batches, add the turkey slices and cook, turning once, until lightly browned and heated through, about 2 minutes.

Spread the bread with the mayonnaise. Top 4 slices with the turkey, tomato, and lettuce, then with the remaining 4 slices of bread. Cut into halves and serve immediately.

Patti's Pointers: Be sure to tell the delicatessen not to slice the smoked turkey too thin! When you bite into the sandwich, it should remind you of hand-sliced smoked ham—and the paper-thin stuff most delis try to sell you won't do it.

Magnificent Meat Dishes

Child, That's Good Cheap Pot Roast!

Like a lot of my special recipes, my Aunt Hattie Mae gave me this one. One thing she taught me: If you want a roast that melts in your mouth, picking the right cut of meat is important. Chuck and bottom round (rump) make the best pot roast. Top round can turn out a little on the dry side.

This mouthwatering recipe is for meat lovers who prefer the meat in a light sauce with the vegetables cooked on the side.

Makes 4 to 6 servings

2 tablespoons all-purpose flour
One 4-pound boneless beef roast, such as chuck or
    bottom round (rump)
¼ cup vegetable oil or shortening
Seasoned salt and freshly ground black pepper
2 medium onions, chopped
1 medium green bell pepper, seeded and chopped
One 1.1-ounce envelope dehydrated beef and
    onion soup mix
2 cups water
1 bay leaf

Preheat the oven to 325°F.

Spread the flour on a plate, and roll the roast in the flour to coat on all sides.

In a Dutch oven, heat the oil over medium-high heat. Add the roast and cook, turning occasionally, until browned on all sides, about 10 minutes. Season with salt and pepper to taste. Transfer to a plate and set aside.

Add the onions and green pepper to the Dutch oven and cook until softened, about 5 minutes. Return the roast to the Dutch oven. Sprinkle the top with half

of the soup mix, turn over, and sprinkle with the remaining soup. Pour the water over the roast, and add the bay leaf. Bring to a simmer.

Cover tightly and bake, turning occasionally, until the roast is very tender, about 2½ hours. Transfer the roast to a carving board and let stand 5 minutes.

Skim off the fat from the surface of the gravy. Discard the bay leaf. Carve the roast and return to the pot. Serve from the pot, with the gravy.

My best friend, Norma, and my niece, Stacye, tell everybody the Patti's-plastic-containers rule: You gotta return them in less than 48 hours, or I'll come looking for you!

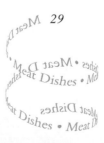

Pass-It-On Pot Roast

When I was growing up, Sunday dinner at our house was a sacred tradition. And not just for my family—for the whole neighborhood. We lived right across the street from the Beulah Baptist Church where my sisters and I were baptized and, on the second Sunday of each month, I sang in the Young Adults Choir.

I can't describe how special those Sundays were to me. From sun up to sun down, I was in sweet ecstasy. Monday through Saturday I sang into a hairbrush in

front of my imaginary friends, but on Sundays I sang in church in front of real people: Chubby, Naomi, my sisters, the man I would one day marry, and half the neighborhood worshiped at Beulah. On those Sunday mornings, carried by the music—the gospel in all its glory—we found ourselves and God.

After Sunday-morning worship, it seemed like the whole congregation came over to our house. From morning until night, there was always a steady stream of friends and neighbors dropping by. As soon as you hit the front steps, you could smell the feast—and that's exactly what it was—that Chubby and Naomi always prepared.

Cookin' with love before company arrives.

If I close my eyes, I can see it. The fried chicken sizzling in black cast-iron pans. The pot roast and potatoes slowly roasting in their juices. The kettles of collard greens and ham hocks simmering on the stove. The cobblers—at least three different kinds—fresh out of the oven.

Unlike a lot of other families, we never had a formal dinner hour. Dishes were set out on card tables that stretched all the way across the living room, and you just helped yourself to whatever you wanted whenever you wanted it. My parents' Saturday-night card parties were invitation only, and homemade dinners

sold for a dollar a plate. But, on Sundays, everything was free and everyone was welcome. On Sundays, it didn't matter how many folks you showed up with, two or twenty-two, no one was ever turned away.

That's why I named this dish "Pass-It-On Pot Roast." When I cook it, I invite lots of folks over and tell them to bring plenty of friends. It's my way of re-creating the Sunday dinners of my youth that taught me food is sometimes the best way to say "welcome."

Makes 6 to 8 servings

One 4-pound boneless beef roast, such as chuck or
    bottom round (rump)
¼ teaspoon seasoned salt, plus more to taste
¼ teaspoon freshly ground black pepper, plus more
    to taste
½ cup all-purpose flour
¼ cup vegetable oil
3 medium onions, 1 chopped and
    2 cut into quarters
1 medium green bell pepper, chopped
2 cups water
2 cups beef broth
4 medium celery ribs, cut into
    2-inch lengths
12 baby carrots or 4 medium
    carrots, cut into 3-inch lengths
8 small red potatoes, scrubbed but unpeeled

Preheat the oven to 325°F. Season the beef with ¼ teaspoon salt and ¼ teaspoon pepper. Place the flour in a shallow plate, and roll the beef in the flour to coat, shaking off the excess. Set the remaining flour aside.

In a Dutch oven, heat 2 tablespoons of the oil over medium-high heat. Add the beef and cook, turning occasionally, until browned on all sides, about 10 minutes. Transfer the meat to a plate and set aside.

Add the remaining 2 tablespoons of oil to the pot and heat. Add the chopped onion and green pepper and cook, stirring occasionally, until tender, about 5 minutes. Return the meat to the pot. Add 1 cup of the water and all the broth. Bring to a simmer. Reduce the heat to medium-low and cover.

Bake, occasionally turning the roast, for 2 hours. Add the quartered onions, celery, carrots, and potatoes. Continue baking until the meat is tender, about 30 minutes.

Remove from the oven. Using a slotted spoon, transfer the roast and the vegetables to a serving platter and cover with foil to keep warm. Skim the fat from the surface of the cooking liquid. Transfer ¼ cup of the reserved flour to a medium bowl. Gradually stir in the remaining 1 cup of water to dissolve the flour. Stir into the pot and bring to a simmer over medium heat. Reduce the heat and simmer until the gravy thickens, about 5 minutes. Season with salt and pepper to taste.

Carve the roast. Return the sliced roast and the vegetables to the pot and simmer for 5 minutes. Serve hot.

Patti's Pointers: This pot roast has a thick brown gravy and plenty of vegetables. It's completely different from the Child, That's Good Cheap Pot Roast! (page 28).

Luscious Liver and Onions

This dish almost got me kicked out of Caesar's Palace. Arsenio Hall was opening for me and, since it was his debut in the famed Circus Maximus showroom, I told him to come up to my suite after the show for a celebration dinner. I know Boyfriend thought I was going to order room service, but he had a surprise coming. I will never forget the look on his face when I pulled out my pans and spread out my groceries. You would have thought I had told him that at the next show I was going to perform a medley of Beach Boys hits wearing nothing but my fever pumps.

"You're not going to cook in here, are you, Patti?" Arsenio sputtered.

Of course, that's exactly what I did. And you can't eat liver and onions without some steamed rice and smothered cabbage, right? So I whipped up a pan of those, too.

I had just gone into the bedroom to get a bottle of hot sauce from my secret stash when I heard this loud banging on the door. I thought it was my hairdresser/traveling companion/best friend, Norma, coming by for dinner and so I told Arsenio to open the door.

With Arsenio Hall, trying to act innocent the night I almost burned down Caesar's Palace.

When he did, it was my turn to be surprised. Standing in the entry to my suite was a six-foot-five-inch hotel security guard.

"Is something wrong, Sugar?" I asked him.

What was wrong, he informed me, was that I had set off the hotel's fire alarms. He cut a quick glance at my smoking pans, then said evenly, "Miss LaBelle, you can't cook in here."

I could tell by the tone in his voice that this was a serious offense, so I started talking a mile a minute.

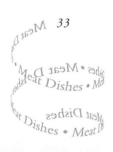

"I'm sorry, Baby. I didn't mean to cause a fuss. What can I do to make it right? Can't we just open a window and keep this between us?"

The security guard took a deep breath: "Well, Miss LaBelle," he said hesitantly, "if you promise not to cook anything else for the rest of your stay . . ."

"I promise," I said, cutting him off before he could change his mind. "And, to show my appreciation, why don't you let me fix you a nice big plate?"

I hope you enjoy the recipe as much as the three of us did that night.

Makes 4 to 6 servings

¼ cup vegetable oil
1 large onion, thinly sliced
2 pounds sliced calves' liver, patted dry with paper
   towels
½ teaspoon salt, plus more to taste
¼ teaspoon freshly ground black pepper, plus more
   to taste
½ cup all-purpose flour
2 cups beef broth or water

In a large skillet, preferably cast-iron, heat 2 tablespoons of the oil over medium heat. Add the onion. Cook, uncovered, stirring occasionally, until golden, about 8 minutes. Transfer to a plate and set aside.

Add the remaining 2 tablespoons of oil to the skillet and heat. Season the liver with ½ teaspoon salt and ¼ teaspoon pepper. Place the flour in a shallow dish. Dip each slice of liver in the flour to coat on both sides, shaking off excess flour. Reserve the flour. Cook until the underside is browned, about 3 minutes. Turn and brown the other side, about 3 more minutes. Transfer to a plate.

Return the onions to the skillet. Sprinkle with 2 tablespoons of the reserved flour and stir well. Stir in the broth and bring to a simmer. Return the liver to the skillet and cover. Simmer until the liver is well done, about 20 minutes. (If you like, cook about 12 minutes for medium-rare liver, and 15 minutes for medium.) Season the sauce with salt and pepper to taste. Serve immediately.

Salsa Meat Loaf

Makes **4 to 6** servings

2½ pounds ground round (85% lean)
½ cup bottled thick hot or medium-hot salsa, plus
    more for serving
½ cup chopped onion
½ cup seeded and chopped green bell pepper
⅓ cup dried bread crumbs
¼ cup chopped green onion, white and green parts
¼ cup finely chopped shallots
2 garlic cloves, minced
2 large eggs, beaten
2 teaspoons salt
1 teaspoon freshly ground black pepper

Preheat the oven to 350°F. Lightly oil a 9 × 5-inch loaf pan.

In a large bowl, combine all of the ingredients with your hands. Mix well, but don't overhandle the mixture or the meat loaf will turn out heavy. Spread evenly in the prepared pan and place on a baking sheet.

Bake until a meat thermometer inserted in the center reads 165°F, about 1½ hours. Cool for 5 minutes before serving. Drain off the pan and unmold onto a serving platter. Slice and serve hot, with more of the salsa on the side.

Patti's Pointers: Use your favorite salsa, as long as it's thick. If you want a milder meat loaf, leave out the salsa. On the other hand, if you want a real kick-in-the-pants loaf, add 1 tablespoon chili powder and ¼ teaspoon ground hot red pepper to the mix. But if you want my real secret to what makes this meat loaf a killer, I think it's using three different kinds of onions.

Righteous Roast Pork

This is another easy recipe that is perfect for company! It's so good, people will think you've been in the kitchen all day.

Makes **6 to 8** servings

3 tablespoons olive oil
2 tablespoons prepared mustard, either yellow or Dijon
1 teaspoon salt, plus more to taste
½ teaspoon freshly ground black pepper, plus more to taste
½ teaspoon crushed red pepper flakes
One 4-pound boneless center-cut pork loin roast
1 tablespoon cornstarch
1 cup beef broth
1 cup half-and-half

Preheat the oven to 350°F. In a small bowl, mix the oil, mustard, 1 teaspoon salt, ½ teaspoon black pepper, and red pepper flakes. Place the roast, fat side up, on a rack in a roasting pan. Brush with half of the mustard mixture.

Bake for 20 minutes. Turn the roast, and brush with the remaining mustard mixture. Continue baking, basting occasionally with the pan drippings, until a meat thermometer inserted in the center of the roast reads 160°F, about 1½ hours. Transfer to a serving platter and let stand while making the gravy.

Pour out and discard the pan drippings, leaving the browned bits in the bottom of the pan. Place the pan over medium heat. In a small bowl, dissolve the cornstarch in ¼ cup of the broth. Stir in the remaining broth. Pour into the pan with the half-and-half. Bring to a simmer, stirring up the browned bits with a wooden spoon. Reduce the heat to medium-low and simmer until thickened, about 3 minutes. Season with salt and pepper. Pour into a sauceboat.

Slice the pork and serve with the sauce passed on the side.

Polynesian Roast Pork with Fruit Sauce

Serve this beautifully glazed roast with Yellow Rice (page 135)—you'll want something to serve with the delicious sauce.

Makes 6 to 8 servings

One 12-ounce can thawed frozen orange-pineapple
   juice concentrate
⅔ cup soy sauce
One 4½-pound center-cut pork loin roast, with bones,
   chine bone removed
⅓ cup chopped green onions, white and green parts
½ teaspoon salt
¼ teaspoon freshly ground black pepper
½ cup raisins
1 medium seedless orange, peeled, cut between
   membranes into sections
1 medium ripe Comice or Anjou pear, peeled, cored,
   and cut into ½-inch cubes
2 teaspoons cornstarch dissolved in 2 tablespoons
   water

In a large plastic bag, mix the orange-pineapple juice concentrate and soy sauce. Add the pork roast. Close the bag and place in a shallow baking dish. Refrigerate, turning often, for 4 hours.

Remove the pork from the bag, reserving the marinade. Using the tip of a sharp knife, make deep slits in the meat between the bones, and stuff with the chopped green onions. Season with the salt and pepper.

Preheat the oven to 350°F. Line a roasting pan with aluminum foil. Place the roast, fat side up, in the pan. Roast for 1 hour. Baste the roast with 3 tablespoons of the reserved marinade. Continue roasting, basting every 10 minutes with the

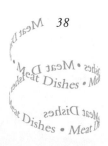

pan drippings, until the roast is glazed and a meat thermometer inserted in the thickest part of the roast reads 160°F, about 40 minutes. Transfer the roast to a serving platter and let stand while making the sauce.

Pour any liquid pan drippings into a glass bowl or measuring cup, discarding the drippings on the foil. Skim off and discard the fat from the surface of the drippings.

In a medium saucepan, bring the raisins and reserved marinade to a boil over high heat. Reduce the heat to medium-low and simmer for 2 minutes. Stir in the orange and pear and cook just to heat through, about 1 minute. Stir in the dissolved cornstarch and return to a boil to thicken the sauce. Pour into a sauceboat.

Carve the roast and serve with the sauce passed on the side.

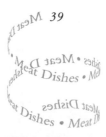

Hellacious Ham with Brown-Sugar Glaze

You've heard of Sunday-go-to-meeting clothes? Well, this is my company's-coming-for-dinner dish. It's so easy to make, I feel guilty accepting all the "oooos and aahhs" it never fails to elicit. In all the years I've been serving this ham, there hasn't been a single time—not one—that I haven't been asked for the recipe. Until now, however, I've kept it a closely guarded secret. For a dinner party or family gathering your guests won't soon forget, serve it with some Better-Than-Mom's Mashed Potatoes and Screamin' Mean Greens (pages 134 and 127). And then sit back and bask in the praise.

Makes 12 to 16 servings

One 7-pound smoked bone-in ham
One 6-ounce can frozen
    orange juice concentrate, thawed
¼ cup packed light brown sugar
¼ teaspoon ground cinnamon
12 whole cloves
Two 8-ounce cans sliced pineapple in juice, drained
    well, juices reserved
8 maraschino cherries, drained

Preheat the oven to 325°F. Line a roasting pan with aluminum foil.

Trim the skin and fat from the ham to leave a ¼-inch layer of fat. Place the ham, fat side up, on a rack in the lined roasting pan. In a small bowl, mix the orange juice, brown sugar, and cinnamon. Spread over the top and sides of the ham.

Roast, uncovered, basting occasionally, for 1½ hours. Remove from the oven. Discard the foil with the scorched pan juices. Line the pan again with fresh aluminum foil. Stud the ham with the cloves and return to the pan. Pour the

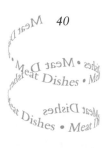

pineapple juice over the ham. Continue baking, basting occasionally, until a meat thermometer inserted in the thickest part of the ham, not touching a bone, reads 140°F, about 30 minutes.

Remove from the oven. To garnish, pierce the cherries with toothpicks. Use the toothpicks to attach the pineapple rings to the ham. Cover loosely with aluminum foil and let stand for 15 minutes.

Patti's Pointers: Bone-in hams have the most flavor, but this glaze works on canned hams, too. Line the pan with aluminum foil for easy cleanup.

Smothered Pork Chops with Mushrooms

Makes 4 servings

2 tablespoons vegetable oil
Four 8-ounce center-cut pork chops with bone
½ teaspoon salt, plus more to taste
¼ teaspoon freshly ground black pepper, plus more to
    taste
1 medium onion, chopped
2 medium celery ribs, chopped
½ medium green bell pepper, seeded and chopped
    (½ cup)
2 garlic cloves, chopped
10 ounces fresh mushrooms, sliced
3 tablespoons all-purpose flour
1½ teaspoons chopped fresh thyme or ½ teaspoon
    dried
1 cup chicken broth or water
1 cup milk
Hot red pepper sauce

In a large skillet, preferably cast-iron, heat 1 tablespoon of the oil over medium-high heat. Season the pork chops with ½ teaspoon salt and ¼ teaspoon pepper. Cook until the underside is browned, about 4 minutes. Turn and brown the other side, about 4 more minutes. Transfer to a plate and set aside.

Add the remaining 1 tablespoon of oil to the skillet and reduce the heat to medium. Add the onion, celery, green pepper, and garlic. Cook, stirring often, until softened, about 3 minutes. Add the mushrooms and cook, stirring often, until they give off their liquid, it evaporates, and they begin to brown, about 8 minutes.

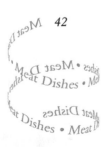

Sprinkle the vegetables with the flour and thyme and stir well. Stir in the broth and milk and bring to a simmer. Return the pork chops and any juices on the plate to the skillet. Reduce the heat to medium–low and cover. Cook, stirring occasionally, until the pork shows no sign of pink when pierced at the bone, 25 to 30 minutes. Season the sauce with the hot pepper sauce. Serve hot.

Patti's Pointers: This dish is terrific served with mashed potatoes.

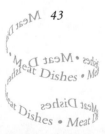

Burnin' Babyback Ribs

I always precook the ribs on top of the stove to season and tenderize them before baking or grilling them with the sauce. Backyard cooks will love this method, as it cooks out most of the fat that usually drips down onto the fire and causes flare-up. I like babyback ribs, but you can use this recipe to prepare spareribs or country-style ribs, if you prefer, allowing an extra 15 minutes to simmer the latter ribs to tenderness.

Makes **4 to 6** servings

4 pounds babyback pork ribs
4 quarts water, approximately
1½ cups cider vinegar
4 teaspoons salt
Freshly ground black pepper
2 cups Bodacious Barbecue Sauce (page 54)

Rinse the ribs under cold running water. Place in a large covered roasting pan. Add 2 quarts water, ¾ cup vinegar, and 2 teaspoons salt. Add more water, if needed, to barely cover the ribs (the tips can stand out of the liquid).

Bring to a simmer over medium heat on top of the stove. Reduce the heat to medium-low and cover. Simmer for 30 minutes. Drain the ribs.

Return the ribs to the pan. Add the remaining 2 quarts water, ¾ cup vinegar, and 2 teaspoons salt, and pepper to taste in the roasting pan, with more water to cover. Bring to a simmer, cover, and cook until the ribs are tender, about 20 minutes. Drain again.

Return the ribs to the pan and pour the sauce over the ribs. Bring to a simmer over medium-low heat. Cover and cook, stirring often so the sauce doesn't stick, until the sauce is thickened and the ribs are glazed, about 10 minutes.

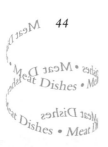

Transfer the ribs to a carving board and cut between the bones into individual ribs. Place the ribs on a serving platter, and pour the sauce in the pan over the ribs. Serve hot.

Backyard Ribs: Build a charcoal fire in an outdoor grill and let burn until the coals are covered with white ash and are medium-hot. (You should be able to hold your hand over the cooking grate for 3 to 4 seconds.) Or, preheat a gas grill on High, then adjust the heat to Medium. Lightly oil the grate.

Drain the ribs after their second simmering. Grill, turning occasionally and basting often with the barbecue sauce, until glazed, about 15 minutes. Serve with the remaining sauce passed on the side.

Sampling a rib to make sure it's just right before my son Zuri takes a platter outside to guests.

Aunt Verdelle's Savory Red Rice with Sausage

Red rice is a close cousin to jambalaya, but it usually has just one meat, instead of jambalaya's chicken, shellfish, and sausage combination. Aunt Verdelle's quick and easy recipe uses hot link sausages.

If you don't have bacon drippings, it's worth cooking up a couple of strips for this recipe. You can crumble the bacon and use it to garnish the rice, if you wish. 𝄞

Helping myself to some of Aunt Verdelle's home cooking.

1 tablespoon bacon drippings or vegetable oil
14 ounces hot link sausage, cut into ½-inch-thick
    rounds
1 medium onion, chopped
1 medium green bell pepper,
    seeded and chopped
2 cups long-grain rice
One 28-ounce can tomatoes in juice, coarsely chopped,
    undrained
2 cups water
¼ teaspoon salt
¼ teaspoon freshly ground
    black pepper
⅛ teaspoon sugar
2 bay leaves

In a Dutch oven, heat the bacon drippings over medium heat. Add the sausage, onion, and green pepper. Cook, stirring occasionally, until the vegetables soften, about 6 minutes. Add the rice and stir well. Stir in the tomatoes with their juices, water, salt, pepper, sugar, and bay leaves. Bring to a simmer.

Reduce the heat to low and cover tightly. Simmer until the rice is tender and has absorbed the liquid, about 20 minutes. Remove from the heat and let stand for 5 minutes. Remove the bay leaves before serving.

Delectable Italian Sausage and Peppers

Makes **4 to 6** servings

2 tablespoons olive oil
1 pound Italian pork sausage, casings removed
1 large onion, sliced
1 large green bell pepper, seeded and cut into
    ½-inch-wide strips
1 large red bell pepper, seeded and cut into
    ½-inch-wide strips
1 large yellow (or another red) pepper, seeded and
    cut into ½-inch-wide strips
2 garlic cloves, minced
One 28-ounce can crushed tomatoes
½ cup water
2 teaspoons dried basil
2 teaspoons dried oregano
¼ teaspoon crushed red pepper flakes
Salt
1 pound spaghetti
Freshly grated Romano cheese

In a large Dutch oven, heat the oil over medium-high heat. Add the sausage. Cook, breaking up the sausage with the side of the spoon into 1-inch chunks, until the sausage is browned, about 10 minutes. Using a slotted spoon, transfer the sausage to paper towels to drain.

Pour off all but 2 tablespoons of the drippings in the skillet. Add the onion, the bell peppers, and the garlic. Cook, stirring occasionally, until the vegetables are softened, about 10 minutes. Stir in the tomatoes, water, basil, oregano, and red pepper flakes. Bring to a boil. Reduce the heat to medium-low. Cook, uncovered, until thickened, about 20 minutes. Season with salt to taste.

Meanwhile, bring a large pot of lightly salted water to a boil over high heat. Stir in the spaghetti. Cook, stirring occasionally, until barely tender, about 9 minutes. Drain well. Serve the spaghetti in individual serving bowls, with the sausage and peppers spooned over the top. Pass the cheese on the side.

Roast Leg of Lamb
with Rosemary-Lemon Rub

The savory combination of lemon zest, rosemary, cayenne pepper, and garlic makes this a memorable roast for a special dinner party. If you have a smaller half leg of lamb, make a half batch of the rosemary-lemon mixture. Serve the roast lamb with Awesome Asparagus and Mouthwatering Mushrooms (pages 122 and 130) and some boiled new potatoes for a menu that's hard to beat.

Relaxing in my new kitchen (check out the fireplace!) with my friend, designer extraordinaire Michael Harrell, as he tries to talk me into giving him my (until now!) secret recipe for roast leg of lamb.

One 7-pound leg of lamb, hipbone section removed
1 large garlic clove, cut into about 20 slivers
2 tablespoons olive oil
2 cups dry white wine
Grated zest of 2 lemons
2 tablespoons chopped fresh rosemary or 1½ teaspoons dried
¾ teaspoon salt
¼ teaspoon freshly ground black pepper
¼ teaspoon ground hot red (cayenne) pepper
1 cup beef broth

Preheat the oven to 350°F. Using a sharp knife, trim all extraneous fat from the lamb. Using the tip of the knife, pierce slits into the lamb, inserting a garlic sliver into each slit. Place on a rack in a roasting pan. Rub the oil over the lamb. Pour 1 cup of the wine over the lamb. In a small bowl, combine the lemon zest, rosemary, salt, black pepper, and red pepper. Rub all over the lamb.

Roast, allowing about 15 minutes per pound, until a meat thermometer inserted in the thickest part of the lamb reads 130°F (for medium-rare lamb), about 1 hour, 45 minutes. (Roast to 140°F for medium lamb, about 2 hours, and 150°F for well–done, about 2 hours, 15 minutes.) About every 20 minutes, baste the lamb with the pan juices and the remaining 1 cup of wine.

Transfer the lamb to a serving platter. Let stand for 10 minutes. Pour the pan juices into a liquid measuring cup. Skim the fat from the surface. Place the roasting pan over medium–high heat. Add the degreased drippings and the beef broth. Bring to a boil, scraping up the browned bits. Cook for 1 minute. Pour into a sauceboat.

Carve the lamb and serve with the sauce.

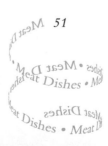

Perfect Poultry

Best-Ever Barbecue Chicken with Bodacious Barbecue Sauce

Makes **6** servings (2 cups sauce)

SAUCE
1 tablespoon vegetable oil
1 garlic clove, minced
One 14-ounce bottle ketchup (1¼ cups)
2 tablespoons light brown sugar
2 tablespoons yellow mustard
2 tablespoons Worcestershire sauce
2 tablespoons cider vinegar
1 tablespoon hot red pepper sauce
1 tablespoon fresh lemon juice
¼ teaspoon ground hot red (cayenne) pepper
½ teaspoon Liquid Smoke

5 pounds chicken drumsticks and thighs
2 tablespoons olive oil
Salt and freshly ground black pepper

To make the sauce: Heat the oil in a medium, heavy-bottomed saucepan over medium heat. Add the garlic and cook, stirring, until fragrant, about 1 minute. Stir in the ketchup, brown sugar, mustard, Worcestershire sauce, vinegar, hot pepper sauce, lemon juice, and ground red pepper. Bring to a simmer, stirring. Reduce the heat to very low. Cook at a simmer, stirring often to avoid scorching, about 15 minutes. Remove from the heat and stir in the Liquid Smoke. Use immediately, or cool completely, cover, and refrigerate for up to 5 days.

To prepare the chicken, preheat the oven to 375°F. Rinse the chicken under cold water and pat dry with paper towels. Arrange the chicken in a single layer in

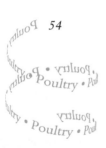

a large roasting pan. Brush with the olive oil and season with salt and pepper to taste. Cover tightly with aluminum foil. Bake for 45 minutes.

Pour off the fat from the pan. Spread the sauce over the chicken. Return to the oven and bake, uncovered, until the chicken is glazed and shows no sign of pink when pierced at the bone, about 15 minutes.

Transfer the chicken to a large platter. Stir the sauce and juices in the pan together, and pour over the chicken. Serve hot.

Backyard Barbecued Chicken: Build a charcoal fire in an outdoor grill and let the coals burn down until covered with white ash and medium-hot (you should be able to hold your hand over the coals for about 3 seconds.) If using a gas grill, preheat on High, then adjust the temperature to Medium. Bake the chicken for 45 minutes and remove from the oven. Grill the chicken, basting often with the barbecue sauce, until glazed, about 15 minutes.

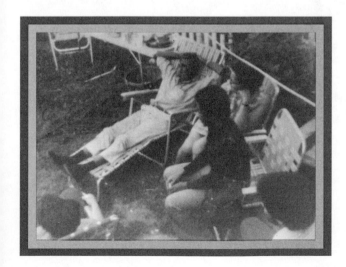

My father-in-law, Percy Edwards, chills out at a backyard cookout while Armstead, my mother-in-law, and I try in vain to talk him into trying my barbecue chicken. "If Anna didn't cook it," he always said, "I don't eat it."

Sumptuous and Simple Southern Fried Chicken

When I was around 10 years old, I went on a chicken strike. It lasted less than a week but, for those few days, I wouldn't let a piece of chicken pass my lips.

My chicken strike had nothing to do with their taste. It was a friendship thing. You see, the chickens were my playmates. At least they were in the summertime. When school let out, Chubby always took my sisters and me down south to Florida to visit my grandparents' farm. For a city kid, it was a wonderland. Except for the outhouse, I loved everything about it. Especially playing with the chickens.

My nephew Billy trying to sweet talk me out of the biggest piece of fried chicken.

One day, when I was heading home from the watermelon patch, I heard this frantic squawking. When I got close enough to see what all the commotion was about, I almost fainted. To my horror, Grandmother Ellen had one of my favorite chickens, and she was wringing its neck.

"Grandmother Ellen," I screamed. "Stop, stop! You're going to kill the chicken."

"Of course I am, child," she said, snapping its neck and spitting a long arc of tobacco juice across the yard. "What do you think we're having for dinner tonight?"

Needless to say, that night I went to bed hungry. And a few more nights after that one, too. Pretty soon, though, my hunger pangs won out over my friendship with the chickens.

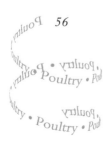

In one of those funny twists of fate, fried chicken has become one of my specialties. My family says I make it so good, it puts the Colonel to shame.

If I had to choose the one person in the family who loves my fried chicken the most, I'd have to say it's my nephew Billy. I'm ashamed to admit it but I bribe him with it all the time. An hour or so before his shift ends at the video store where he works, I call him up.

"Bring me the hot new movie tonight, Sugar, and I'll cook you some fried chicken."

A few hours later, I'm sitting on the sofa watching the movie, and Billy's sitting in the kitchen eating chicken.

I can't take the credit for this fabulous fried chicken, I'm afraid. Both the recipe and the technique are at least three generations old. I learned how to fry chicken like Southern cooks—crisp on the outside, juicy on the inside—by watching my mother. And she learned it from the master chicken swinger-plucker-fryer: Grandmother Ellen.

After you've cooked up a batch, bite into your favorite piece and savor the crusty-on-the-outside, juicy-on-the-inside result. 🎼

Makes 4 servings

One 3- to 3½-pound chicken, rinsed and cut into 8 pieces
(or use your favorite chicken part)
½ teaspoon salt, plus more to taste
¼ teaspoon freshly ground black pepper, plus more to taste
1 cup all-purpose flour
2 large eggs
Vegetable oil, for deep-frying

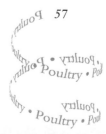

Line a baking sheet with paper towels.

Season the chicken with ½ teaspoon salt and ¼ teaspoon pepper. Place the flour in a large paper bag (or large bowl) and season with salt and pepper. In a medium shallow bowl, beat the eggs. One piece at a time, dip the chicken in the eggs, shake (or roll) in the flour to coat completely, and place on a baking sheet.

Pour enough oil into a large skillet, preferably cast-iron, to come one-third up the sides. Heat over high heat until very hot but not smoking. (If using an electric skillet, heat to 365°F.) Using tongs, carefully add the chicken. Fry the chicken, uncovered, turning occasionally with the tongs, until the chicken is golden brown on all sides and shows no sign of pink when pierced in the thickest part (don't turn down the heat unless the chicken is browning too quickly). Breasts and wings will cook in about 15 minutes, and the drumsticks and thighs will take about 20 minutes. An instant-read thermometer, inserted in the thickest parts of the chicken, will read 170°F. Transfer to the paper towels to drain. Serve hot.

Patti's Pointers: Don't forget that white meat takes less time to cook than dark, so it should be removed from the skillet first.

And don't try to squeeze a big chicken into the skillet—3½ pounds is the max. To be sure it will fit, put the drumsticks and thighs in first, then the breasts. If the wings won't fit, let the chicken in the skillet cook for 5 minutes; it will shrink enough to make space for the wings.

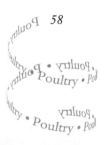

Succulent Roast Chicken

No one makes me feel better about my cooking than my nephew Michael. I don't care if Mike has just eaten a four-course meal. If he hears I'm home and I'm cooking, he'll come straight over to the house and eat a second time.

That's exactly what happened the last time I made roast chicken. Mike called the house looking for Zuri, and I told him he had to hold a second while I put the chicken in the oven. Why did I do that?

"I'm on the way over, Aunt Pat," he said, and gave me Mr. Click.

Fifteen minutes later, Mike was sitting at my kitchen table waiting for the chicken to come out of the oven.

A few weeks later, he confessed. "I had just eaten dinner, Aunt Pat. Spaghetti, salad, French bread, the works. But I had to come over and eat again. With your tour schedule, who knew when I'd get a chance to have some of your cooking again?"

Sampling some goodies I cooked for my nephew Michael after his graduation from American University.

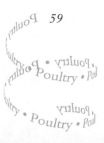

One 6½-pound roasting chicken
1 teaspoon poultry seasoning
½ teaspoon seasoned salt
¼ teaspoon freshly ground black pepper
4 tablespoons (½ stick) butter, melted
½ cup water

Preheat the oven to 375°F. Remove the giblets from the chicken and rinse under cold running water. Pat the giblets dry with paper towels. Rinse the chicken well, inside and out, under cold running water. Pat the chicken dry with paper towels, being sure to dry the body cavity, too.

Place the chicken on a rack in a roasting pan just large enough to hold the chicken. Place the giblets in the pan. Season the inside of the chicken with ½ teaspoon of the poultry seasoning, ¼ teaspoon of the salt, and ⅛ teaspoon of the pepper. Place on the rack. Pour the melted butter over the chicken. Season the outside of the bird with the remaining ½ teaspoon of poultry seasoning, ¼ teaspoon salt, and ⅛ teaspoon pepper.

Roast, uncovered, basting with the pan juices every 15 minutes, until a meat thermometer inserted in the thickest part of the thigh reads 170°F, about 1 hour, 45 minutes. As the giblets are cooked and tender, remove them and place on a plate: The liver will take about 45 minutes, and the other giblets about 1 hour, 15 minutes.

Transfer the chicken to a serving platter. (I like to soak up the juices in the cavity with a paper towel.) Pour the pan juices into a glass bowl or liquid measuring cup. Skim off the fat from the surface. Place the roasting pan over

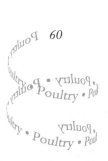

medium-high heat and heat until sizzling. Add the water and the skimmed drippings to the pan, and scrape up the browned bits on the bottom of the pan. Bring to a boil and cook for 1 minute. Finely chop the reserved giblets and stir into the gravy. Pour into a sauceboat. Carve the chicken and serve with the giblet gravy.

Patti's Pointers: Even if you don't feel like using the giblets in the gravy, roast them along with the chicken anyway—they add lots of flavor to the pan drippings.

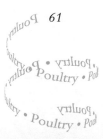

Say-My-Name Smothered Chicken and Gravy

There is only one person I know who can pluck a chicken as clean and as fast as my Grandmother Ellen. Chubby Checker. Before he became a famous recording star, Chubby worked at Henry Colt's, the poultry market near our house where my mother did her Saturday-morning grocery shopping.

Of course, he wasn't Chubby Checker back then. Dick Clark's wife had yet to change his name because she thought he was a cute version of Fats Domino. ("Fats" became "Chubby" and "Domino" turned into "Checker.")

When I met Chubby Checker, he was Ernest Evans, the cutest, pudgiest, fastest chicken-plucker in Philly. He was also a big part of the reason I loved grocery shopping with Chubby. Before Ernest went in the back of the store to clean and pluck your chicken, he would entertain you with jokes and songs and impersonations.

"I don't have time for that today," Chubby would tell Ernest when he would go on a little too long. "I'm making smothered chicken for dinner tonight, and I have to get home and get it started."

"No problem Mrs. Holte," Ernest would say and disappear in the back with our dinner. We could barely get over to the produce section before Ernest was back with the cleanest chicken I've ever seen. Next to Grandmother Ellen's, of course.

To this day, making smothered chicken takes me back to those Saturday-morning shopping sprees with Chubby and Chubby.

Hungry yet?

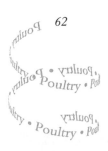

Makes **4** servings

One 3½-pound chicken, rinsed and cut into 8 pieces
½ teaspoon salt, plus more to taste
¼ teaspoon freshly ground black pepper, plus more to taste
1 cup all-purpose flour
½ cup vegetable oil
2 medium onions, chopped
2 medium celery ribs, chopped
1 garlic clove, minced
3 cups chicken broth

Season the chicken with ½ teaspoon salt and ¼ teaspoon pepper. Place the flour in a large bowl. Roll the chicken in the flour to coat, shaking off excess flour. Transfer 3 tablespoons of the flour to a medium bowl and set aside.

In a large skillet, heat the oil over medium–high heat. Add the chicken and cook, turning halfway during cooking, until golden brown, about 10 minutes. Transfer to a plate and set aside.

Pour off all but 3 tablespoons of the oil from the skillet. Reduce the heat to medium. Add the onions, celery, and garlic and cook, stirring often, until tender, about 5 minutes. Sprinkle with the reserved flour and stir well. Gradually stir in the broth and bring to a simmer.

Return the chicken to the skillet. Reduce the heat to low. Cover and simmer, stirring occasionally, until the chicken is cooked through and shows no sign of pink when pierced at the bone, about 35 minutes. Transfer the chicken to a deep platter and cover with foil to keep warm. Bring the sauce to a boil over high heat and cook, stirring often, until thickened, about 5 minutes. Season the gravy with salt and pepper and pour over the chicken. Serve hot.

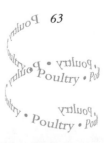

Old-Fashioned Chicken and Dumplings

When it came to making dumplings, my mother wasn't just an expert; she was an artist. On weekends, she and Daddy used to throw card parties and, in between games of poker and pitty pat, Chubby and Naomi sold homemade dinners. Fried chicken and potato salad went for around a dollar a plate. If you wanted greens, they were extra.

Some nights, for a special treat, Chubby would pass around bowls of her chicken and dumplings. "Bertha, honey," folks used to say. "You got your M.D., girl." M.D., of course, stood for master dumpling maker.

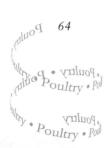

A soul food feast prepared by my Aunts Hattie and Joshia Mae. When I was a girl growing up in Philly, this is just the way the table used to look every Sunday when Chubby and Naomi fed the whole neighborhood.

Chubby's dumplings were so good, in all the years Naomi lived with us, they were the only thing I ever heard them argue about.

"Naomi, do you think you could try not to eat all the dumplings out of the pot this time?" Chubby would say.

"That depends. Do you think you could try not to be so stingy with them this time?" Naomi would counter.

Given my mother's dumplings skill, you would think I could make a mean one. God clearly has a sense of humor because I can't make a good dumpling to save my life. I am so dumpling impaired, in fact, whenever I make this dish, I have to get Armstead to make the dumplings. That's not a complaint, mind you. His are as good as Chubby's!

With a little luck and a little practice, this dish just might channel her spirit into your kitchen.

Makes **6 to 8** servings

One 5- to 6-pound stewing hen (see Patti's Pointers)
½ teaspoon seasoned salt, plus more to taste
¼ teaspoon freshly ground white or black pepper, plus
    more to taste
2 quarts water, approximately
Two 10¾-ounce cans cream of chicken soup
2 medium onions, quartered
4 medium celery ribs, cut into 2-inch lengths
2 medium carrots, cut into ½-inch-thick rounds, optional

DUMPLINGS

2 cups self-rising flour
½ teaspoon salt
½ cup milk

Chopped fresh parsley, thyme, or chives

Rinse the hen well, inside and out, with cold running water. Season the hen well, inside and out, with ½ teaspoon seasoned salt and ¼ teaspoon pepper.

In a large pot, mix 2 quarts water, the soup, onions, celery, and carrots, if using. Place the hen in the pot, breast side down, adding more water to barely cover the hen, as needed. Bring to a boil over high heat, skimming off any foam that rises to the surface.

Reduce the heat to medium-low and simmer, covered, turning the hen occasionally, until very tender, 2½ to 3 hours. Lift the hen from the pot and transfer to a platter. Keep the cooking liquid at a low simmer. Skim the clear yellow fat from

the surface of the broth. Reserve ½ cup of the fat, and discard the remainder. Let the chicken and reserved fat cool until the chicken is easy to handle, 20 to 30 minutes. Remove and discard the skin and bones, cut the meat into bite-sized pieces, and return the meat to the pot.

To make the dumplings: In a medium bowl, stir the flour and salt. In a small bowl, mix the reserved fat and the milk. (If the fat is still hot, stir in an ice cube to cool it down.) Stir into the flour to form a stiff dough. Knead in the bowl to gather up the dough, and pat or roll out into a 7-inch square about ½ inch thick. Using a sharp knife, cut into 20 dumplings. Transfer the dumplings to a baking sheet.

Season the cooking liquid with salt and pepper to taste. One at a time, drop the dumplings into the simmering liquid. Cover tightly and simmer until the dumplings are cooked through, 15 to 20 minutes.

Spoon the chicken, vegetables, and dumplings into bowls, sprinkle with parsley, and serve hot.

Aunt Hattie Mae's Stewed Chicken: Delete the dumplings. Make the chicken exactly the same way, but use only one can of cream of chicken soup. This is excellent served with Beyond-Good Bacon and Buttermilk Corn Bread (page 204).

Fluffy Dumplings: Skim the fat from the surface of the cooking liquid and discard; do not reserve. In a medium bowl, mix the flour and salt. Using a pastry blender or two knives, cut in ½ cup vegetable shortening until the mixture resembles fine crumbs. Stir in about 1 cup milk to make a stiff dough (you may not need all of the milk). Gather up the dough and roll out into an 8-inch square about ½ inch thick. Cut into 24 dumplings. Simmer the dumplings as directed.

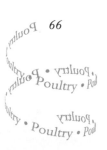

Patti's Pointers: The best stewed chicken with the richest, most mouthwatering broth is made from a long-simmered, big, old stewing hen (also known as a fowl). Look for stewing hens at Latino, Asian, and other ethnic markets, and poultry stores. If necessary, substitute one 5- to 6-pound roasting chicken for the hen, and simmer until falling-apart tender, about 1½ hours.

This recipe uses the rendered chicken fat skimmed from the top of the broth to make tasty, firm-textured dumplings. If you like light and fluffy dumplings, make the Fluffy Dumplings variation.

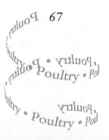

Chicken Brunswick Stew

When my Great Grandmother Mariah made Brunswick stew, she used a hog's head instead of chicken! Be sure and crush the crackers as finely as possible so they dissolve easily to thicken the sauce.

Makes **6 to 8** servings

One 6-pound roasting chicken
4 medium all-purpose potatoes, peeled and cut into 1-inch cubes
One 15-ounce can diced tomatoes in juice, undrained
2 medium onions, chopped
2 cups fresh or frozen corn kernels (see Note, page 18)
One 9-ounce box frozen lima beans
One 14-ounce bottle ketchup (1¼ cups)
1½ cups finely crushed soda crackers (about 1 chute, 30 crackers)
2 tablespoons cider vinegar
Hot red pepper sauce
Salt and freshly ground black pepper

Rinse the chicken well. Place in a large pot and add lightly salted cold water to cover by 2 inches. Cover and bring to a boil. Skim off any foam. Reduce heat to low and simmer, covered, until the meat falls off the bone, about 1½ hours. Transfer the chicken to a platter. Remove and discard the skin and bones. Chop the meat and set aside.

Strain the broth into a large bowl. Skim most of the fat from the surface. Place the potatoes, tomatoes with their juice, onions, corn, and lima beans in the pot. Add broth to cover the vegetables. Bring to a boil over high heat. Reduce the heat to medium and simmer for 10 minutes. Stir in the reserved chicken, ketchup, crackers, and vinegar. Cook, stirring often, until the sauce is thick and the potatoes are tender, about 10 more minutes. Add hot pepper sauce, salt, and pepper to taste. Serve hot.

Zuri's Favorite Buffalo Wings with Blue Cheese Dip

This is the one and only dish my youngest son, Zuri, ever asks me to cook for him. Unlike the rest of my family, Z is just as happy eating at McDonald's as he is eating at his Mama's.

Four years ago, when Zuri turned 21, Armstead and I wanted to do something special to mark the moment. We decided to throw him a huge pool party and invited 200 of his closest friends over to the house. I wanted this milestone, this rite of passage in my baby's life, to be perfect. And so, while I had the other food catered, Zuri's Buffalo Wings I made myself. Uh-hummm, yep, that's right: I stayed up until four o'clock in the morning cooking 500 of those things. What can I say? That's what happens when you have motherlove inside you.

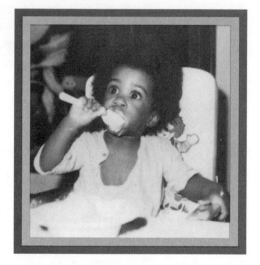

I can't prove it, but I'm convinced Zuri's nonchalant attitude about my other dishes goes all the way back to his infant days. The first few weeks of his life, Zuri cried all the time. I don't mean like normal babies. I mean *all* the time. I tried everything I knew to comfort him—holding him, rocking him, singing to him, nursing him. Nothing worked. Nothing I did could quiet him.

Zuri, age 1, after he finally got something nutritious to eat!

Finally, the doctors figured out what the problem was. My milk. It didn't contain the right nutrients. Zuri cried all the time the first few weeks of his life because the poor little thing was starving! As soon as we put him on formula, the crying stopped. Zuri became a healthy and happy little baby. But somewhere way down deep in his subconscious I think he associates his mother's milk with his mother's food.

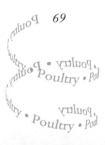

BLUE CHEESE DIP

3 ounces blue cheese
3 tablespoons milk
½ cup mayonnaise
½ cup sour cream
1 tablespoon fresh lemon juice
1 teaspoon celery seed
¼ teaspoon freshly ground black pepper

3 pounds chicken wings (see Patti's Pointers)
Vegetable oil, for deep-frying
3 tablespoons butter
3 tablespoons hot red pepper sauce, such as Crystal
   or Durkee's

To make the dip: In a small bowl, mash the blue cheese with the milk until creamy and not too lumpy. Stir in the mayonnaise, sour cream, lemon juice, celery seed, and pepper. Cover and refrigerate for 30 minutes before serving.

Preheat the oven to 200°F. Line a baking sheet with paper towels. Wash the chicken wings and pat dry with paper towels. Using a cleaver or heavy knife, chop the wings between the joints into 3 pieces, and discard the wing tips.

Pour enough oil into a large skillet, preferably cast-iron, to come halfway up the sides. Heat over high heat until very hot and shimmering, but not smoking. (If using an electric skillet, heat to 365°F.) In batches without crowding, fry the chicken wings, turning with tongs halfway through, until golden brown, about 5 minutes. Transfer to paper towels and keep warm in the oven while frying the remaining wings.

Meanwhile, in a small saucepan, melt the butter over low heat. Add the hot sauce and cook, stirring constantly, until heated through, about 1 minute.

Place the chicken wings in a large bowl. Add the butter mixture and toss well. Serve hot with the dip on the side.

Patti's Pointers: Despite their labels, a lot of "hot" sauces are actually pretty mild (the original recipe from the Anchor Bar in Buffalo reportedly uses Durkee's, but Frank's and Crystal are also not too hot).

"Buffalo-style" chicken wings (first and second joints only, with no wing tips) are available at many supermarkets and wholesale clubs. Or, if you wish, use chicken wing drumettes.

Baked Turkey Wings with Onion Sauce

My mother-in-law, Anna Edwards, gave me this delicious recipe. Long-cooking makes the onions "melt" into a delicious, and easy, sauce.

Makes 4 servings

Four 1½-pound turkey wings, rinsed and patted dry
1 teaspoon dried thyme
1 teaspoon poultry seasoning
½ teaspoon salt, plus more to taste
¼ teaspoon freshly ground black pepper, plus more to
   taste
2 large onions, chopped
2 cups chicken broth
Perfectly Steamed Rice (page 135)

Preheat the oven to 350°F.

Arrange the turkey wings in a single layer in a large roasting pan. Season all over with the thyme, poultry seasoning, ½ teaspoon salt, and ¼ teaspoon pepper.

Sprinkle the chopped onions over the turkey wings and season with salt and pepper to taste. Pour in the broth. Cover tightly with aluminum foil.

Bake until the wings are tender, about 1 hour, 45 minutes. During the last 15 minutes, remove the foil so the wings brown lightly. Using a slotted spoon, transfer the wings and onions to a serving platter. Skim off the fat from the cooking liquid and pour over the turkey and onions. Serve hot, with the rice.

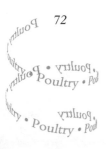

Too-Good-to-Be-Turkey Chili

One of the best compliments I have ever gotten about my cooking comes from my son Stanley. He says when he was in college, my turkey chili made him Mr. Popularity. The first year Stanley was away, like all mothers, I worried about him eating right. And so, more than a few times, when he came home on a break, I sent him back to school with enough food to feed half his dorm.

By his second year, Stanley says that word had spread among his friends that his mom was a serious down-home, makes-you-wanna-holler-and-throw-up-both-your-hands cook. Sometimes, when he returned to school from a trip home, his friends would be lined up at his dorm room waiting to see what goodies he might be bringing back. More than once a disappointed latecomer had to be satisfied with stories about my chili, because the real thing was long gone.

Teaching my son Stanley and his friend Michele how to make his favorite turkey chili.

As much as Stanley loves my chili, it's not his favorite dish. He reserves his highest praise for my potato salad (see page 6). "I don't eat anybody else's," he says. "Every now and then, when I think that's too rigid a rule, I take a chance and sample somebody else's potato salad. Invariably, I regret it. Then some time will pass and again I'll tell myself my no-foreign-potato-salad rule is a little too undemocratic and again I open myself to cautious experimentation—with the predictably disastrous results."

For now, Stanley says, his rule is firmly reinstated.

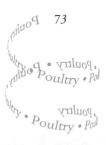

2 tablespoons vegetable oil
2 pounds ground turkey (see Patti's Pointers)
2 medium onions, chopped
1 small green bell pepper, seeded and chopped
1 jalapeño or ½ habanero chile pepper, seeded and
    minced, or more to taste (see Patti's Pointers)
2 garlic cloves, minced
3 tablespoons chili powder
2 teaspoons ground cumin
1 teaspoon dried oregano
½ teaspoon ground hot red (cayenne) pepper
2 cups water
One 14½-ounce can diced tomatoes, with juice
One 15-ounce can crushed tomatoes
One 6-ounce can tomato paste
Seasoned salt and freshly ground black pepper

In a Dutch oven, heat the oil over medium-high heat. Add the ground turkey, onions, green pepper, jalapeño, and garlic. Cook, stirring occasionally, until the turkey loses its pink color, about 10 minutes. Stir in the chili powder, cumin, oregano, and ground red pepper and cook for 1 minute. Add the water, tomatoes with their juice, crushed tomatoes, and tomato paste, stirring well to dissolve the paste. Bring to a simmer.

Reduce the heat to medium-low. Simmer uncovered, stirring occasionally, until slightly thickened, about 1 hour. Season with salt and pepper to taste. Serve hot.

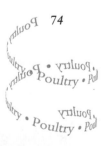

Patti's Pointers: Use regular ground turkey, not ground turkey breast meat (99% lean), to make the tastiest, juiciest chili. Ground skinless turkey breast is just too lean to make a good pot of chili, as it dries out if cooked too long.

When you're feeling indulgent, top with sour cream, shredded cheese, crumbled tortilla chips, chopped onions, or sliced olives.

And, if you like your chili as hot as I do, use the habanero pepper. However, be warned: Habaneros are only for real chile heads. No pretenders! Start with half a habanero, and add more, if you like, but only after tasting the pot of chili first. Just to give you an idea of the difference between a habanero and a jalapeño, you should know about the Scoville heat unit, a method of determining a chile's heat developed by a pharmacist in 1912. The Scoville unit analyzes the amount of capsaicin (the ingredient that causes the heat) in chile peppers by measuring how much alcohol and sugar water it takes to completely dilute the taste. A jalapeño has between 2,500 and 5,000 heat units. Cayenne has about 30,000 units. And habanero has 200,000 to 300,000!

Cornish Hens with Shallot Cream Gravy

Makes 4 servings

Four 1½-pound Cornish hens
1 teaspoon poultry seasoning
1 teaspoon seasoned salt
¼ teaspoon freshly ground black pepper, plus more
    to taste
4 tablespoons (½ stick) butter, melted
⅓ cup chopped shallots
2 tablespoons all-purpose flour
2 cups chicken broth
2 tablespoons heavy cream
Salt
Perfectly Steamed Rice (page 135)

Preheat the oven to 350°F. Rinse the hens well, inside and out, with cold running water. Pat the hens dry with paper towels.

In a small bowl, combine the poultry seasoning, seasoned salt, and ¼ teaspoon pepper and season the hens inside and out with the mixture. Place the hens in a shallow roasting pan. Pour the melted butter over the hens. Bake, basting occasionally with the pan drippings, until the hens show no sign of pink when pierced at the thigh bone, about 1½ hours.

Transfer the hens to a platter and cover loosely with foil to keep warm. Pour the pan drippings into a glass bowl. Skim off and reserve 2 tablespoons of fat from the surface of the drippings, discarding the remaining fat. Reserve the drippings.

Return the 2 tablespoons of fat to the roasting pan and heat over medium heat. Add the shallots and cook, stirring, until softened, about 2 minutes. Sprin-

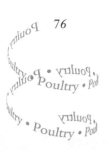

kle with the flour and stir until the flour is lightly browned, about 1 minute. Stir in the broth, reserved drippings, and cream. Bring to a simmer. Reduce the heat to low. Simmer, stirring often, until thickened, about 3 minutes. Season with salt and pepper. Pour into a sauceboat. Serve the hens, with the sauce and steamed rice.

The-Spirit's-in-It Spaghetti with Meaty Tomato Sauce

Makes 4 to 6 servings

SAUCE

2 tablespoons olive oil
1 pound ground turkey
    (not ground turkey breast)
1 pound Italian-style turkey sausage, cut into 1-inch
    chunks
1 large onion, chopped
3 garlic cloves, minced
One 28-ounce can crushed tomatoes
Two 6-ounce cans tomato paste
2½ cups water
3 tablespoons chopped fresh basil or 2 teaspoons dried
2 tablespoons chopped fresh oregano or 2 teaspoons
    dried
½ teaspoon crushed red pepper flakes
Salt

1 pound spaghetti
Freshly grated Parmesan or Romano cheese

To make the sauce: In a Dutch oven, heat the oil over medium-high heat. Add the ground turkey and turkey sausage. Cook, breaking the turkey up well with a spoon, until it loses its raw look, about 10 minutes. Add the onion and garlic and cook until the onion softens, about 5 minutes. Stir in the tomatoes, tomato paste, water, basil, oregano, and red pepper flakes. (If using fresh herbs, stir them in during the last 10 minutes of cooking.) Bring to a simmer. Reduce the heat to medium-low. Cook, uncovered, stirring occasionally, until slightly thickened, about 40 minutes. Season with salt to taste.

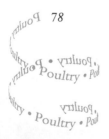

Meanwhile, bring a large pot of lightly salted water to a boil over high heat. Add the spaghetti and cook, stirring occasionally, until barely tender, about 9 minutes. Drain well.

Transfer the spaghetti to a serving bowl. Top with half of the sauce and serve immediately, with the cheese passed on the side.

Patti's Pointers: This makes enough sauce for 2 pounds of pasta, so save half of the sauce and freeze it for another meal. I like cooking this with fresh herbs, but dried herbs work well, too.

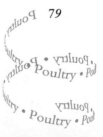

Lasagna LaBelle

SAUCE

2 tablespoons olive oil, plus more for pan
1 large onion, chopped
3 garlic cloves, minced
1 pound ground turkey
 (not ground turkey breast)
1 pound Italian-style turkey sausage, casings removed
1 cup water
One 28-ounce can crushed tomatoes
One 6-ounce can tomato paste
2 teaspoons dried oregano or 2 tablespoons chopped
 fresh
3 tablespoons chopped fresh cilantro
Salt and freshly ground black pepper

1 pound lasagna noodles
1 tablespoon olive oil, optional
1½ cups (6 ounces) shredded mozzarella cheese
1½ cups (6 ounces) shredded provolone cheese
One 15-ounce container ricotta cheese

Preheat the oven to 350°F. Grease a 13 × 9-inch dish with olive oil.

To make the sauce: Heat the oil in a Dutch oven over medium heat. Add the onion and garlic and cook, stirring often, until the onion is tender, about 5 minutes. Add the ground turkey and turkey sausage and cook, breaking up the turkey well with a spoon, until it loses its raw look, about 10 minutes. Stir in the water, crushed tomatoes, tomato paste, and dried oregano. (If using fresh oregano, stir it into the finished sauce with the cilantro.) Bring to a simmer. Reduce the heat to medium-low. Cook, uncovered, stirring occasionally, until slightly thickened, about 30 minutes. Stir in the cilantro. Season with salt and pepper to taste.

Meanwhile, bring a large pot of lightly salted water to a boil over high heat. One at a time (to keep them from sticking), add the lasagna noodles to the pot. Cook, stirring occasionally, until barely tender, about 8 minutes. Do not over-cook—the noodles will cook again in the oven. Drain well and rinse under cold running water. If not using immediately, toss with 1 tablespoon olive oil.

In a medium bowl, combine the mozzarella and provolone cheeses; set aside.

Spread a thin layer of the sauce on the bottom of the prepared dish. Line the dish with a layer of overlapping noodles, cutting the noodles to fit, if needed. Top with one-fourth of the sauce, one-third of the shredded cheese, and one-third of the ricotta. Repeat with two more layers of noodles, sauce, shredded cheese, and ricotta. Finish with a layer of noodles, spread with sauce. Cover with aluminum foil.

Bake for 30 minutes. Uncover and bake for 15 more minutes. Remove from the oven and let stand for 10 minutes. Cut into squares to serve.

Patti's Pointers: You may have a few extra noodles, but that's fine because some of them may break during cooking. The lasagna can be assembled, covered, and refrigerated up to 8 hours ahead. Add an extra 15 minutes to the covered baking time if chilled.

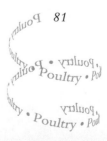

Omelet Patti Cake

Makes **4 to 6** servings

3 small red potatoes, scrubbed, but unpeeled
1 tablespoon butter
8 ounces smoked turkey kielbasa, cut into ½-inch dice
6 shiitake mushrooms, stems removed, chopped (about ¾ cup)
4 green onions, white and green parts, chopped
8 large eggs
3 tablespoons milk
½ teaspoon salt
⅛ teaspoon freshly ground black pepper
⅛ teaspoon ground hot red (cayenne) pepper
1 cup (4 ounces) shredded Monterey Jack cheese
2 tablespoons chopped fresh basil or oregano

Place the potatoes in a medium saucepan and add enough cold lightly salted water to cover by 1 inch. Bring to a boil over high heat. Reduce the heat to low and simmer until tender, about 20 minutes. Drain and rinse under cold water until easy to handle. Cut into ½-inch dice. Set aside.

Preheat the oven to 375°F. In a 10-inch ovenproof nonstick skillet, melt the butter over medium heat. Add the kielbasa, mushrooms, and green onions. Cook, uncovered, stirring occasionally, until the mushrooms give off their liquid and it evaporates, about 10 minutes. Stir in the potatoes.

In a large bowl, beat the eggs, milk, salt, pepper, and ground red pepper until well combined. Stir in the cheese. Pour into the skillet. Cook, lifting up the edges of the omelet with a rubber spatula, letting the uncooked portion run underneath, until the edges are set, about 2 minutes.

Bake in the oven until the eggs set, about 10 minutes. Sprinkle with the herbs. Cut into wedges, and serve hot.

Scrumptious Seafood

Perfect Pan-Fried Fish Fillets

Since I'm not a sun-and-sand kind of girl (I can't stand heat and I can't swim a lick), there are only two things about our beach house in the Caribbean that I can honestly say I love. The first is spending quiet time with Armstead in sublime seclusion. The second is the fish.

Since Armstead became a fish-eating vegetarian back in the seventies, I've learned to cook all kinds of fish—from blackfish to bluefish, tuna to trout. But it was in Eleuthera that I fell in love with fish. The fish on this island have the aroma of the sea. The first time Armstead brought some home, I went nuts. I ate so much you would have thought I had never had a piece of fresh fish in my life.

By midafternoon the next day, I was down at the docks. Now, there are very few things I will stand outside in the hot sun for. A good shoe sale and the fish on this island are the only two things that come to mind. Whenever I go there, come 2:30 in the afternoon, everybody on the island knows where to find me: down at the docks, lined up with the locals waiting to see my dinner being hauled off the fishing boats.

After the fishermen clean my selections, I head home and fry them up like this. Lately, I've also been using Armstead's Caribbean-inspired recipe for grilled fish (see page 86).

Fish lovers know, the fresher the fish, the better the taste, so when making your selections, let yourself be inspired by the freshest catch in the market.

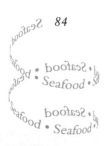

Makes **4 servings**

1½ pounds fish fillets (see Patti's Pointers), cut into
   4 to 6 pieces
½ teaspoon salt
¼ teaspoon freshly ground black pepper
¾ cup yellow cornmeal
½ cup vegetable oil
Lemon wedges

Rinse the fillets under cold running water and shake off excess water. Season with the salt and pepper. Place the cornmeal in a shallow dish. Coat the fillets on both sides with cornmeal. Set aside on a baking sheet.

In a large skillet, preferably cast-iron, heat the oil over medium-high heat until hot, but not smoking. Add the fillets. Cook until the underside is golden brown, 2 to 3 minutes. Turn carefully, and cook until the other side is golden brown, 2 to 3 more minutes. Transfer to paper towels to drain briefly.

Serve hot, with the lemon wedges.

Patti's Pointers: These crispy, crunchy, golden brown fillets are usually served with Down-Home Hush Puppies (page 208). Use any fish fillet you like—catfish, sea bass, flounder, porgy, or whiting. The exact cooking times depend on the thickness of the fillet. Thin flounder or sole fillets will cook in 4 minutes, but thicker fillets like snapper or catfish will take 6 minutes.

Grilled Caribbean Fish Steaks

The honey and soy sauce combine to give the fish a nice mahogany-colored glaze. You can use fish fillets or steaks, but steaks are much easier to deal with because they won't break up when turned. Tuna, swordfish, and salmon steaks, cut about ¾ inch thick, all work well. If you want to grill fillets, stick to salmon, snapper, and striped bass. In any case, be sure the grill is well greased—hold a wad of paper towels with long-handled tongs, dip in vegetable oil, and wipe over the grilling grate. This is a *terrific* all-purpose marinade—it would be just as tasty on pork chops or boneless chicken breasts. Just don't use it with anything that takes longer than 30 minutes to cook, or the glaze could scorch.

Armstead feigning exhaustion after cooking a family feast. I have to admit, Boyfriend can burn!

Makes **4 to 6** servings

⅓ cup fresh lime juice
¼ cup honey
¼ cup soy sauce
¼ cup vegetable oil
2 garlic cloves, chopped
¼ teaspoon seeded and minced habanero chile pepper, or
　more to taste
⅛ teaspoon freshly ground black pepper
2 pounds fish fillets or steaks (see recommendations
　above), cut into individual portions
Lime wedges

In a glass baking dish, mix the lime juice, honey, soy sauce, vegetable oil, garlic, habanero chile, and black pepper. Add the fish and turn to coat with the marinade. Cover with plastic wrap and refrigerate for 1 hour, turning the fish occasionally in the marinade. Do not overmarinate, or the lime juice will start to "cook" the fish.

Build a charcoal fire in an outdoor grill. Let the fire burn until the coals are covered with white ash and are medium-hot—you should be able to hold your hand at grate level to a count of three. If using a gas grill, preheat on High, then adjust the heat to Medium.

Remove the fish from the marinade. Oil the grilling grate well. Grill the fish, turning once, until the fish looks opaque when flaked in the thickest part with the tip of a knife, about 6 minutes for fish fillets and 8 minutes for fish steaks. Serve hot with the lime wedges.

Quick Linguine with Clam Sauce

For a quick supper, this is hard to beat. The secret is a little butter, which really gives the sauce a better flavor than olive oil alone.

Makes 4 to 6 servings

Four 6½-ounce cans minced clams
1 pound linguine
2 tablespoons butter
1 large onion, finely chopped
3 garlic cloves, minced
2 tablespoons chopped fresh basil
2 tablespoons chopped fresh oregano
¼ teaspoon crushed red pepper flakes, or more to taste
⅓ cup olive oil, preferably extra virgin
Salt and freshly ground black pepper

Drain the clams, reserving the juice. Set the clams aside.

Bring a large pot of lightly salted water to a boil, adding the clam juice to the water. Add the pasta and cook, stirring occasionally, until just tender, about 9 minutes.

While the water is coming to a boil and the pasta is cooking, make the sauce: In a large nonstick skillet, heat the butter over medium heat. Add the onion and garlic and cook until the onion is golden, about 5 minutes. Stir in the clams, basil, oregano, and red pepper flakes and reduce the heat to medium-low. Cook, stirring often, just until the clams are heated through, about 5 minutes.

Drain the pasta well. Return to the warm pot and toss with the oil. Add the clam mixture and toss again. Season with salt and pepper to taste. Transfer to individual serving bowls and serve hot.

Make-You-Wanna-Holler Maryland Crab Cakes

You've heard of "Bring-You-Money Greens"? Well, I thought about calling this recipe "Get-a-Husband Crab Cakes." I can't swear to it, but I'm pretty sure this recipe helped me win my husband.

As many of you know, Armstead asked me to marry him more than once before I said "yes." Even when I finally accepted his proposal, I wouldn't set a wedding date. For almost two years, every time Armstead asked me to pick a date, I stalled.

And then one day, after I'd put him off for the umpteenth time, he said: "Pat, you will never have to worry about me asking you to marry me again."

And, true to his word, he didn't. He did, however, change his attitude about our relationship. Slowly but surely I could feel Armstead pulling away from me.

"I think I've lost him," I told Sarah and Nona, one day after I'd called him and he had sounded particularly distant.

"Well, Pat," they advised me, "if you think he's never going to propose to you again, you propose to him."

Giving how-to-pick-a-crab-clean lessons to my sister-friend Cassie.

And that's exactly what I did. We were at Armstead's apartment when I popped the question.

"I have something important to ask you," I said, my voice trembling. "Will you marry me?"

Armstead's answer stunned me. "I don't know, Pat. I need some time to think about it."

I was shaken, but I tried to be cool. "Okay," I said. "No pressure; take all the time you need."

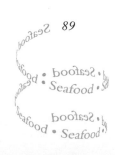

The next day, I did what I always do when I'm upset and I need to cool myself out. I cooked. Early in the morning, I was at the seafood market picking out all of Armstead's favorites. That night, I fixed us a seafood feast. Armstead enjoyed everything, but there's one dish I'm convinced tipped the balance in my favor: my Make-You-Wanna-Holler Maryland Crab Cakes. Armstead ate three!

The next day, he said "yes" to my marriage proposal, although he made me wait all day for his answer. Five days later—on July 23, 1969—we eloped. People tell me it's just a coincidence that we got married in Maryland, the state famous the world over for its jumbo lump crab cakes. But they didn't see Armstead eating mine. 🎼

Makes 4 servings

3 tablespoons butter
¼ cup finely chopped onion
1 pound jumbo lump crabmeat, picked over to remove
   cartilage
⅓ cup fresh bread crumbs (see Patti's Pointers)
1 large egg, lightly beaten
¼ teaspoon hot red pepper sauce
Seasoned salt and freshly ground pepper
Lemon wedges

In a medium skillet, heat 1 tablespoon of the butter over medium heat. Add the onion. Cook, stirring occasionally, until tender, about 4 minutes. Transfer to a medium bowl.

Add the crabmeat and sprinkle on the bread crumbs. Pour the egg and hot pepper sauce on top. Season with salt and pepper to taste. Using your hands, gently mix, being careful not to break up the crabmeat any more than necessary.

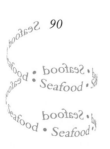

Form the mixture into 6 patties, about 3 inches in diameter. Place on a wax paper–lined baking sheet. Cover with plastic wrap and refrigerate for 1 hour (this helps the crab cakes hold together).

Position the rack about 6 inches from the source of heat and preheat the broiler. Lightly grease the broiler pan. In a small saucepan, melt the remaining 2 tablespoons of the butter. Place the crab cakes in the broiler pan and brush the tops with the melted butter.

Broil the crab cakes until the tops are golden brown, about 4 minutes. Turn and continue broiling until the other side is golden brown, about 4 more minutes. Serve hot, with the lemon wedges.

Patti's Pointers: Use fresh bread crumbs, made in a blender or food processor from crustless firm white sandwich bread, not dried bread crumbs from a box. The best crab cakes are lumpy with big chunks of crabmeat, so don't stir the mixture so much that they break apart. Crab cakes are supposed to taste like crab, not bread, so I use the absolute minimum amount—just enough to keep the cakes from falling apart. I prefer broiling the cakes to frying because the flavor of the crab doesn't have to compete with the flavor of the cooking oil. When forming your crab cakes be sure to sprinkle the bread crumbs over the crabmeat and then pour the egg and hot sauce on top. And, last but not least, don't compact the crab cakes too tight.

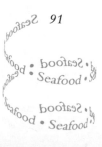

Have-to-Have-'Em Hard-Shell Crabs

When I was a teenager, there was one sure way to start a fight in my house: bring home a bushel of crabs. The way my three sisters and I fought over crabs, you would have thought they were filled with money, not crabmeat. And I don't just mean we argued over crabs; the four of us had some knock-down-drag-out fights over them.

Our crab feast ritual was always the same. After Chubby steamed the crabs, Vivian, Barbara, Jackie, and I took turns fishing them out of the crab pot and placing them on the picnic table we had lined with newspaper in the backyard. We could only take one crab out of the pot at a time, a rule Chubby had made to ensure we each had an equal shot at getting a few nice big fat ones.

One afternoon, my oldest sister, Vivian, claimed the biggest, fattest crab in the bushel. Naturally, it was the one I had my heart set on eating.

"Patsy," she warned me as she got up to go in the house and get a cold beer. "If you so much as look at that crab while I'm gone, I promise you I will whip your behind."

Of course, the minute Vivian left, I tore that baby up. And the minute she came back outside, Vivian tore me up. I was crying and screaming at the top of my lungs, but Vivian showed no mercy. "You ate my crab," she said, as she was setting my butt on fire, "you pay the price."

Before it was all over, I had a bruise on my behind twice the size of that crab. But, like I told Vivian, that crab was so good, it was worth it.

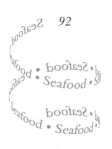

Caught by photographers after a show in Atlantic City showing my sister-friend Cassie how to tell the boy crabs from the girl crabs.

As much as my sisters and I fought over crabs when I was growing up, that's not how this recipe got its name. I dubbed it "Have-to-Have-'Em Hard-Shell Crabs" because of what happened on my wedding day. Neither Armstead nor I wanted a big fancy ceremony, so we decided to elope out of town where Armstead's cousin Joan offered to find us a justice of the peace and let us crash in her guest room for the night.

After the ceremony, we were toasting our future and drinking champagne when it hit me. Not only was I married; I was in Maryland—home of the best hard-shell crabs in America! Of course, I had to have some. *That night.* When I asked Armstead to run out and pick up a dozen, he looked at me like I had lost my mind. "Okay," I said, "but the honeymoon won't start until I have some."

An hour later, Armstead was walking through the door with my crabs. See why I say he's the right kinda lover?

Now, whenever I cook crabs, the smells and the sounds of them steaming in the pot echo summers past when I still had my sisters. But be forewarned: I'll still fight you for the biggest one.

Makes **4 to 6** servings

2 dozen live blue crabs
One 12-ounce can lager beer
1 cup water
1 cup white distilled vinegar
¾ cup Chesapeake Bay–style crab seasoning
1 tablespoon salt
1 teaspoon hot red pepper sauce
2 teaspoons celery seed
1 teaspoon crushed red pepper flakes

Fill a sink with ice water. Add the crabs and let stand for 5 minutes. This numbs the crabs and helps rinse off any sand on their shells.

In a large pot, bring the beer, water, vinegar, ¼ cup of the crab seasoning, the salt, and hot pepper sauce to a boil over high heat. In a small bowl, combine the remaining ½ cup crab seasoning with the celery seed and red pepper flakes.

Using long tongs, place 12 crabs in the pot, first sprinkling them with about half of the seasoning mixture. Cover tightly. Boil until the crabs turn red, about 10 minutes. Using tongs, transfer the crabs to a large platter. Cook the second batch of crabs, sprinkling with the remaining seasoning, while serving the first.

To serve, line the table with newspapers and put out a bowl to collect the shells. Serve the crabs, providing nutcrackers and small mallets for cracking the shells. If your guests don't know how to eat blue crabs, here's how: Break off the large claws and crack with a nutcracker or mallet to get to the meat. Starting at the tip of the "apron" (the triangular or bell-shaped area on the underside of the crab), pull off the top part of the shell from the rest of the body. Break the

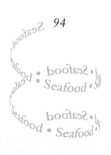

body in half vertically. There's a lot of good meat underneath the inedible, featherlike gills. If your crab has any yellow fat, be sure to eat it—it's delicious.

Patti's Pointers: Chesapeake Bay cooks are famous for their spicy boiled crabs. There are a lot of crab seasonings out there, and the most popular one, Old Bay Seasoning, may not be your favorite after all. Try to find one that isn't too salty.

In my opinion, male crabs are meatier. Usually, the fish store will pick out the crabs for you—that's because they know that savvy buyers will pick out the males! If you have a chance to choose your own, here's how to identify the two sexes. Turn the crab over and look at the "apron" on the underside. Male crabs have triangular-shaped aprons; the aprons are bell-shaped on females.

Serve steamed blue crabs to your best buddies—there will be a lot of licking of fingers and slurping going on at the table. Figure on 4 to 6 crabs per person. For a real Chesapeake feast, serve with Naomi's Creamy Coleslaw (page 4), corn on the cob, and lots of ice-cold beer.

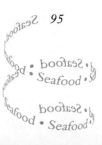

Butterflied Lobster Tails with Herbs and Garlic Butter

This dish looks every bit as good as it tastes! It's so attractive, in fact, when I cook it I have been known to take off my house shoes and apron and put on my fever pumps and diamonds. (Hey, you want your food to look good, you gotta look good, too!) Frozen lobster tails are available at good fish stores. Defrost thoroughly in the refrigerator overnight for the best results. Serve with a green vegetable, like Spectacular Spinach (page 138), steamed new potatoes, and a glass of chardonnay for a very elegant meal.

Armstead and me giving our niece Mikaela her first lesson on how to eat a lobster in public.

Makes **2 to 4** servings

Four 6- to 8-ounce lobster tails
8 tablespoons (1 stick) butter
2 garlic cloves, crushed through a press, or ¼ teaspoon
   garlic powder
2 tablespoons chopped fresh parsley, basil, or oregano
Lemon wedges

In a large saucepan, bring ½ inch of lightly salted water to a boil over high heat. Add the lobster tails and cover tightly. Cook until the shells turn bright red, about 5 minutes. Drain and cool slightly.

Meanwhile, in a small saucepan, melt the butter with the garlic over medium heat. (If using garlic powder, melt the butter, remove from the heat, and stir in the garlic powder.) Pour the garlic butter into small ramekins or dishes for dipping.

Using a kitchen towel to protect your hand from the hot shell, place a lobster tail, hard top shell down, on a work surface. Using a heavy, sharp knife, cut the lobster tail lengthwise, down to, but not through, the hard top shell. Open up the two halves like a book. Repeat with the remaining lobster tails.

Serve immediately, sprinkled with the parsley, with the garlic butter and lemon wedges.

So-o-o Good Salmon Casserole

A recipe that could use a one-pound can of salmon, but is even better (and not much harder) when made from scratch. 🎼

Makes 4 to 6 servings

1 pound salmon fillet
¾ teaspoon salt
¼ teaspoon freshly ground black pepper
1 tablespoon butter
1 small onion, chopped
¼ cup seeded and finely chopped green bell pepper
2 medium celery ribs, chopped
½ cup (2 ounces) shredded mozzarella cheese
½ cup (2 ounces) shredded sharp Cheddar cheese
7 slices firm white sandwich bread, toasted and torn into
 bite-sized pieces
6 large eggs
2½ cups milk
⅛ teaspoon ground hot red (cayenne) pepper

Season the salmon with ½ teaspoon of the salt and ⅛ teaspoon of the pepper. Place in a large skillet and add enough cold water to barely cover the salmon. Bring to a simmer over medium heat. Reduce the heat to medium-low and cover. Cook until the salmon looks opaque when flaked in the center, about 10 minutes. Using a slotted pancake turner, transfer to a plate and cool. Remove the skin and any stray bones from the salmon. Place in a medium bowl and flake well with a fork.

Butter an 8 × 11-inch (2-quart) shallow baking dish.

In a medium skillet, melt the butter over medium heat. Add the onion, green pepper, and celery. Cook uncovered, stirring occasionally, until tender, about 5 minutes.

In a small bowl, combine the mozzarella and Cheddar cheeses. Place one-third of the bread in a layer in the casserole. Sprinkle with half each of the cheese, salmon, and cooked vegetables. Top with half of the remaining bread, then the remaining cheese, salmon, and cooked vegetables. Finish with the remaining bread.

In a medium bowl, beat the eggs. Beat in the milk, ground hot pepper, and remaining ¼ teaspoon salt and ⅛ teaspoon pepper. Pour evenly over the bread. Cover and refrigerate for 2 hours.

Preheat the oven to 350°F. Bake, uncovered, until a knife inserted in the center comes out clean, about 50 minutes. Let stand for 5 minutes before serving hot.

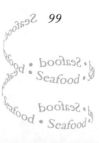

Salmon Croquettes Deluxe

Makes **4 to 6** servings

1 pound salmon fillet
¾ teaspoon seasoned salt
¼ plus ⅛ teaspoon freshly ground black pepper
1 large russet or Idaho potato (about 12 ounces),
    peeled and cut into 1-inch chunks
1 tablespoon milk
1 tablespoon butter
½ cup finely chopped onion
⅓ cup seeded and finely chopped green bell pepper
1 large egg, lightly beaten
½ cup dried bread crumbs
½ cup vegetable oil
Lemon wedges

Season the salmon with ½ teaspoon of the salt and ⅛ teaspoon of the pepper. Place in a large skillet and add enough cold water to barely cover the salmon. Bring to a simmer over medium heat. Reduce the heat to medium-low and cover. Cook until the salmon looks opaque when flaked in the center, about 10 minutes. Using a slotted pancake turner, transfer to a plate and cool.

Meanwhile, place the potato in a medium saucepan and add enough lightly salted water to cover. Bring to a boil over high heat. Reduce the heat to medium and cook until tender, about 15 minutes. Drain well. Return to the pot. Add the milk and butter and mash with a potato masher. Cool completely.

Remove the skin and any stray bones from the salmon. Place in a medium bowl and flake well with a fork. Add the cooled mashed potatoes, onion, green pepper, and egg. Season with the remaining ¼ teaspoon salt and ¼ teaspoon pepper. Place the bread crumbs in a shallow dish. Using about ⅓ cup for each, form

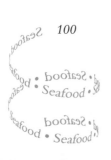

the salmon mixture into 8 patties. Coat with the bread crumbs, shaking off the excess, and transfer the croquettes to a plate.

In a large skillet, preferably cast-iron, heat the oil over medium-high until hot, but not smoking. Add the croquettes and cook until the underside is golden brown, about 3 minutes. Turn and cook until the other side is golden brown, about 3 more minutes. Transfer to paper towels to drain briefly. Serve hot, with the lemon wedges.

Patti's Pointers: This dish is great with canned salmon from the cupboard, too.

Savory Salmon Steaks

One of the classiest, fastest fish dishes on the planet. These are great summer fare, because you don't have to turn on the oven, and they are terrific cold.

Makes 4 servings

Four 8- to 10-ounce salmon steaks
¼ teaspoon salt
⅛ teaspoon freshly ground black pepper
1 tablespoon olive oil
2 garlic cloves, minced
¼ cup dry white wine, such as Sauvignon Blanc
1 tablespoon fresh lemon juice
2 tablespoons chopped fresh basil or oregano, or a
  combination

Season the salmon with the salt and pepper. Set aside.

In a large skillet, heat the oil over medium heat. Add the garlic and cook until fragrant, about 1 minute. Add the wine and lemon juice and bring to a simmer. Add the salmon and cover. Simmer until the salmon looks opaque when flaked with the tip of a knife, 12 to 15 minutes.

Using a slotted spatula, transfer the salmon to a platter. Sprinkle with the chopped basil and serve immediately.

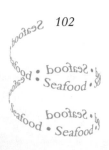

Sardines Sublime

I fell in love with sardines back in the sixties. And when I say love, I mean *love*. Many a day canned sardines were the only thing that kept Sarah, Nona, Cindy, and me from starving. And that's no exaggeration.

Back in the sixties, when we were touring the country as Patti LaBelle and the Bluebelles, the four of us performed back-to-back one-nighters in a different city just about every night. It wasn't unusual for us to do two and three shows a day, then pile into our manager's beat-up station wagon and drive to the next show in the next city.

Of course, in those days a lot of restaurants wouldn't serve Black people. And so, to keep from going hungry, we had to bring our own rations. Wherever we went, we had to make sure we packed enough food—crackers, cookies, sardines, anything that didn't have to be cooked or refrigerated—to carry us through to someplace that would serve us. Especially when we were touring in the Deep South. In the Deep South, who knew how long we would have to drive before we found a restaurant where we could eat.

It sounds unbelievable now but Cindy, Sarah, Nona, and I had some of our worst arguments over canned sardines. Somebody was always accusing somebody else of hoarding them or hiding them. Or, the worst crime of all, eating more than her fair share. More than thirty years later, I can't fix this dish without thinking about those long-ago days.

I discovered this way of preparing sardines when I was touring Europe. In

At least there was one advantage to the food-rationing lifestyle: Check out the bodies on Cindy, Sarah, Nona, and yours truly!

Europe, broiled sardines are served as an appetizer. The first time I tasted them prepared this way, I told the waiter, "Hold my entrée, Sugar, and just bring me three of these!" I swear, that's how good they were.

Of course, as soon as I got back to the States, I was in the kitchen re-creating this dish Patti style. Be adventurous. Try it; I think you'll like it.

Makes 4 servings

12 to 16 large sardines, cleaned
4 tablespoons (½ stick) butter
1 garlic clove, minced
2 tablespoons fresh lemon juice
¼ teaspoon salt
¼ teaspoon freshly ground black pepper
2 tablespoons chopped fresh cilantro, oregano, or parsley
Lemon wedges

Position a broiler rack about 4 inches from the source of heat and preheat the broiler.

Rinse the sardines well, inside and out, under cold running water. Pat dry with paper towels.

In a small saucepan, melt the butter with the garlic over medium heat until the garlic is sizzling and fragrant. Remove from the heat and stir in the lemon juice.

Brush the sardines with the garlic butter and place them in a broiler pan or flameproof baking dish. Season with the salt and pepper. Reserve the remaining garlic butter.

Broil until the tops of the sardines are lightly browned, about 3 minutes. Carefully turn and continue broiling until the other side is browned, about 3 more minutes. If the sardines are too delicate to turn, don't bother, but move them farther away from the source of heat so they don't burn. Pour the reserved garlic butter over the sardines and sprinkle with the cilantro. Serve hot, with lemon wedges.

Patti's Pointers: This is a recipe for fish lovers. You'll be eating the moist, succulent flesh off of the bone, so if you don't like dealing with bones, make another recipe. The only catch here is to find fresh, whole sardines. If they aren't gutted, you can ask the fish store to do them for you, or clean them yourself: Using a small, sharp knife, slice the underbelly lengthwise. With the tip of the knife, scrape out the innards. Rinse the inside of the sardines well under cold running water.

Sardines are excellent grilled outdoors. Just be sure to brush both sides well with the garlic butter, and oil the grilling grid well, too, so they won't stick. The sardines will cook in 6 to 8 minutes.

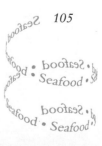

Butterflied Shrimp with Double Dips

Deep-fried shrimp are another easy and delicious supper dish. It's fun to make a couple of quick dips for the shrimp. Make the dips first so the flavors can blend. Use the biggest shrimp you can afford, but not the jumbo ones.

Makes **4** servings

GOOD AND SPICY COCKTAIL SAUCE

½ cup prepared American-style chili sauce
1 tablespoon prepared horseradish
1 tablespoon fresh lemon juice
Hot red pepper sauce

LADY MARMALADE SAUCE

½ cup orange marmalade
2 tablespoons Dijon mustard
1 garlic clove, crushed through a press

2 pounds extra-large (26/30 per pound) shrimp
Vegetable oil, for deep-frying
3 large eggs
1 cup all-purpose flour
Salt and freshly ground black pepper

To make the cocktail sauce: Combine all of the ingredients in a small bowl. Cover and let stand at room temperature for 1 hour.

To make the marmalade sauce: In a small saucepan, melt the marmalade over low heat. Stir in the mustard and garlic. Let stand in a warm place until ready to serve.

Preheat the oven to 200°F. Peel and devein the shrimp, keeping the tail segment intact. To butterfly the shrimp, using a small, sharp knife, cut into the deveining incision of each shrimp, cutting almost, but not completely, through to the underside. Open up the shrimp like a book.

Pour enough oil into a large skillet, preferably cast-iron, to come halfway up the sides. Heat over medium-high heat until the oil is very hot, but not smoking. (If using an electric skillet, heat to 365°F.)

In a medium bowl, beat the eggs. Place the flour in another medium bowl. Frying the shrimp in 2 or 3 batches, dip the shrimp in the egg, and then coat with the flour, shaking off the excess flour. Fry until golden brown, about 3 minutes. Using a skimmer or slotted spoon, transfer the shrimp to a paper towel–lined baking sheet and keep warm in the oven while frying the remaining shrimp.

Season the fried shrimp with salt and pepper to taste. Serve hot, with the dips.

My son Zuri (age 7) and his buddy Donald learning how to clean and butterfly shrimp.

Clear-Out-Your-Sinuses Super-Spicy Steamed Shrimp

Simple, simple, simple, and good, good, good. Serve with Patti's Potato Salad and Beyond-Good Bacon and Buttermilk Corn Bread (pages 6 and 204). ♪

Makes 4 servings

One 12-ounce can lager beer
1 cup distilled white vinegar
1 cup water
1 tablespoon hot red pepper sauce
1 teaspoon ground hot red (cayenne) pepper
2 garlic cloves, minced
2 pounds large to extra-large (31/35 to 26/30 per
    pound) shrimp, unshelled
Lemon wedges

In a Dutch oven, bring the beer, vinegar, water, red pepper sauce, ground red pepper, and garlic to a boil over high heat. Add the shrimp. Cook, uncovered, stirring occasionally, until the shrimp are pink and firm, about 3 minutes.

Drain in a colander over a large bowl. Transfer the shrimp to a large platter. Serve with the lemon wedges and a bowl of the cooking liquid to use as a dip.

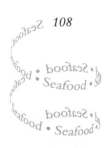

Shrimp Étouffée

This wonderful seafood dish features shrimp swimming in a classic Creole sauce. (Étouffée means "smothered," which these shrimp are.) Serve over steamed rice to sop up every last bit of the sauce.

Makes 4 to 6 servings

6 tablespoons (¾ stick) butter
1 large onion, chopped
4 medium celery ribs, chopped
4 green onions, white and green parts, chopped
½ cup chopped fresh parsley
3 garlic cloves, minced
1 teaspoon poultry seasoning
½ teaspoon crushed red pepper flakes
⅛ teaspoon ground hot red (cayenne) pepper
3 tablespoons all-purpose flour
2½ cups chicken broth
1 tablespoon fresh lemon juice
1½ pounds large shrimp, peeled and deveined
Salt
Perfectly Steamed Rice (page 135)

In a large nonstick skillet, melt the butter over medium heat. Add the onion and celery. Cook, stirring occasionally, until tender, about 5 minutes. Add the green onions, parsley, garlic, poultry seasoning, red pepper flakes, and ground red pepper and cook until the garlic is fragrant, about 2 minutes.

Sprinkle with the flour, then stir well. Stir in the broth and lemon juice. Bring to a simmer. Reduce the heat to low and simmer for 10 minutes. Stir in the shrimp and cook until pink and firm, about 5 minutes. Season with salt to taste. Serve hot, spooned over the rice.

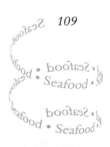

Slammin' Shrimp Creole

Makes 4 to 6 servings

¼ cup vegetable oil
¼ cup all-purpose flour
¾ cup chopped onions
½ cup chopped green onions, white and green parts
2 celery ribs, chopped
½ cup seeded and chopped red bell pepper (or use ¼ cup
    each green and red bell pepper)
1 garlic clove, minced
3 cups chicken broth or water
One 15-ounce can chopped tomatoes, undrained
One 8-ounce can tomato sauce
One 6-ounce can tomato paste
½ teaspoon dried oregano
½ teaspoon dried basil
½ teaspoon dried thyme
½ teaspoon ground hot red (cayenne) pepper
1 bay leaf
2 pounds large (31/35 per pound) shrimp, peeled and
    deveined
Yellow Rice (page 135)
¼ cup chopped fresh cilantro
Salt and freshly ground black pepper

In a heavy large skillet, preferably cast-iron, heat the oil over medium heat. Gradually stir in the flour. Cook, stirring almost constantly, until the roux turns dark brown, about 8 minutes. The roux should smell toasty, but don't let it burn!

Stir in the onions, green onions, celery, bell pepper, and garlic. Cook, stirring often, until the vegetables are softened, about 8 minutes. Stir in the chicken broth, tomatoes with their juices, the tomato sauce, tomato paste, oregano, basil,

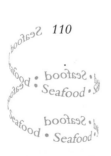

thyme, ground red pepper, and bay leaf. Bring to a simmer. Reduce the heat to low and simmer, stirring occasionally, for 1 hour.

Stir in the shrimp. Cook until the shrimp are pink and firm, about 5 minutes. Remove the bay leaf. Serve hot, spooned over the Yellow Rice, sprinkling each serving with cilantro. Season with salt and pepper to taste.

Caught in the act! My nephew Robert, Jr. tries to sneak some shrimp off the plate of his son Robert III at a family feast.

Jammin' Jambalaya

Here's a really excellent jambalaya with lots of flavor.

Makes 6 to 8 servings

4 tablespoons vegetable oil
1 pound boneless, skinless chicken breast, cut into
    ¾-inch pieces
1 teaspoon salt
¼ teaspoon freshly ground black pepper
1 pound andouille, hot links, or kielbasa sausage, cut
    into ½-inch pieces
1 large onion, chopped
4 medium celery ribs, chopped
1 medium green bell pepper, seeded and chopped
1 medium red bell pepper, seeded and chopped
2 garlic cloves, finely chopped
1 teaspoon dried thyme
½ teaspoon chili powder
½ teaspoon crushed red pepper flakes
½ teaspoon ground hot red (cayenne) pepper
1 bay leaf
2 cups long-grain rice
4 cups chicken broth
1 large ripe tomato, seeded and chopped
1 pound large (31/35 per pound) shrimp, peeled
    and deveined
2 green onions, white and green parts, chopped

In a Dutch oven, heat 2 tablespoons of the oil over medium-high heat. Season the chicken with ½ teaspoon of the salt and all the black pepper. Cook, stirring occasionally, until lightly browned, about 5 minutes. Transfer to a plate and set aside.

Add 1 tablespoon of oil to the pot and heat. Add the sausage and cook, stirring occasionally, until lightly browned, about 5 minutes. Using a slotted spoon, transfer to the plate with the chicken.

Add the remaining 1 tablespoon of oil to the pot and heat. Add the onion, celery, green and red bell peppers, and garlic and cover. Cook, stirring often, until tender, about 10 minutes. Stir in the remaining ½ teaspoon salt, and the thyme, chili powder, red pepper flakes, ground red pepper, and bay leaf. Add the rice and stir well. Stir in the chicken broth and the tomato, then the reserved chicken and sausage. Bring to a boil. Cover and reduce the heat to medium–low. Simmer for 15 minutes. Stir in the shrimp, cover, and continue cooking until the rice absorbs the liquid and the shrimp are pink and firm, about 5 minutes. Remove from the heat and let stand for 5 minutes. Remove the bay leaf. Serve immediately, sprinkling each serving with green onions.

Serious Shrimp Fried Rice

Makes 4 to 6 servings

3 tablespoons vegetable oil
3 large eggs
2 green onions, white and green parts, chopped
¼ cup chopped shallots
2 garlic cloves, finely chopped
1 pound large (31/35 per pound) shrimp, peeled and
    deveined, coarsely chopped
3 tablespoons soy sauce
4 cups cooked rice, well chilled
1½ cups bean sprouts (6 ounces)
½ cup thawed frozen peas
Crushed red pepper flakes
3 tablespoons chopped fresh cilantro

In a large nonstick skillet, heat 1 tablespoon of the oil over medium heat. In a medium bowl, beat the eggs until combined. Pour into the skillet and cook, stirring occasionally, until firm, about 1 minute. Transfer to a platter. Coarsely chop the eggs. Set aside.

Wipe out the skillet with paper towels. Add the remaining 2 tablespoons of oil to the skillet. Add the green onions, shallots, and garlic and stir until softened, about 1 minute. Add the shrimp and cook until pink and firm, about 2 minutes. Stir in the soy sauce. Add the rice, bean sprouts, peas, and scrambled eggs. Cook, stirring almost constantly, until the rice is heated through, about 3 minutes. Season with red pepper flakes to taste and sprinkle with the cilantro. Serve hot.

Patti's Pointers: The cooked rice must be chilled for the dish to cook properly.

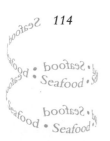

Roasted Red Snapper with Oyster and Mushroom Stuffing

A big red snapper, filled with a rich, luscious stuffing, makes a dramatic entrée for company dinners. (If you can't find a large whole snapper, use the stuffing with snapper fillets.) Serve with a green vegetable like Awesome Asparagus (page 122) and something colorful like Sautéed Summer Squash with Basil (page 143), and sit back and wait for the compliments.

Makes 6 servings

One 6-pound whole red snapper, scaled and gutted
½ teaspoon salt
¼ teaspoon freshly ground black pepper
2 tablespoons butter
2 tablespoons olive oil

STUFFING

5 tablespoons butter
1½ cups finely chopped shiitake mushrooms, without stems
⅓ cup finely chopped onion
⅓ cup finely chopped celery
⅓ cup finely chopped green bell pepper
1 garlic clove, minced
1 teaspoon poultry seasoning
2 tablespoons chopped fresh cilantro or parsley
⅛ teaspoon ground hot red (cayenne) pepper
2 cups (½-inch cubes) firm white sandwich bread, left out to
    dry at room temperature overnight
8 ounces shucked oysters, cut in half if large (about 9 oysters)
¼ cup water
Salt and freshly ground black pepper
Lemon wedges

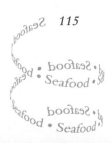

Rinse the fish inside and out with cold running water and pat dry with paper towels. Make three ¼-inch-deep slashes in the thickest parts on both sides of the fish (this helps the fish cook more evenly). Season the fish inside and out with the salt and pepper, being sure to rub some seasonings into the incisions. Place the fish in a large roasting pan and refrigerate while making the stuffing.

In a small saucepan, melt 2 tablespoons butter with the oil over medium heat. Set aside.

To make the stuffing: In a large skillet, heat the 5 tablespoons butter over medium heat. Add the mushrooms, onion, celery, green pepper, and garlic. Cook, stirring occasionally, until the vegetables are tender, about 8 minutes. Transfer to a bowl and stir in the poultry seasoning, cilantro, and ground red pepper. Remove from the heat and stir in the bread and oysters. Stir in the water, mixing until the stuffing is evenly moistened. Season with salt and pepper to taste.

Preheat the oven to 400°F. Remove the fish from the refrigerator. Fill the body cavity with the stuffing, and close the cavity with metal or bamboo skewers. Generously brush the fish with the butter and oil mixture. Cover the pan with aluminum foil.

Bake the fish for 30 minutes. Uncover the fish and baste with the pan juices. Continue baking, uncovered, until the fish is firm and opaque throughout (look in one of the incisions to check) and the stuffing is heated through, about 15 minutes. Remove from the oven and let stand for 5 minutes. Using two large spatulas or pancake turners, lift the fish and place on a large platter.

To serve, use a long, thin knife to cut along the backbone of the fish. Cut the top fillet into 3 portions. Using a spatula, lift the top fillets from the bones and

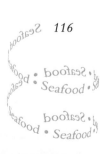

place on individual plates. Lift off and discard the large bone structure. Spoon the stuffing onto the plates. Cut the bottom fillet into 3 portions and serve. Pass the lemon wedges on the side.

Stuffed Snapper Fillets: Substitute six 6- to 8-ounce snapper fillets for the whole snapper. Butter a 15 × 10-inch baking dish. Place the fillets on a work surface and season lightly with salt and pepper to taste. Divide the stuffing equally among the fillets, placing it on the lower half of each fillet. Fold over each fillet to cover the stuffing—the stuffing will not be covered on the sides. Place in the baking dish. Brush with the melted butter/oil mixture and season with salt and pepper. Bake in a preheated 400°F oven until the fish is opaque when flaked with the tip of a knife, about 30 minutes.

Simply Spectacular Seafood Pasta

Makes 4 to 6 servings

1 pound angel hair pasta
3 cups water
6 garlic cloves, chopped
1 teaspoon salt, plus more to taste
3 dozen littleneck clams
6 tablespoons (¾ stick) butter
1 pound medium shrimp, peeled and deveined
1 pound sea scallops, patted dry with paper towels
⅓ cup extra virgin olive oil
2 tablespoons chopped fresh basil
2 tablespoons chopped fresh oregano
¼ teaspoon crushed red pepper flakes, or more to taste
Freshly ground black pepper
2 tablespoons chopped fresh parsley

Bring a large pot of lightly salted water to a boil over high heat. In 2 or 3 batches, stir in the pasta. Cook, stirring occasionally to be sure it doesn't stick together, until al dente, about 3 minutes.

While the water is coming to a boil and the pasta is cooking, make the sauce: In a Dutch oven, bring the water, half of the garlic, and 1 teaspoon salt to a boil over high heat. Rinse the clams under cold running water, scrubbing with a stiff brush to clean the shells. Add to the boiling water and cover. Cook, shaking the pot occasionally, until all of the clams open, 5 to 7 minutes. Discard any clams that have not opened. Remove the pot from the heat and let stand, covered, to keep warm.

Meanwhile, in a large skillet, heat 3 tablespoons of the butter over medium-high heat. Add the remaining garlic and cook for 1 minute. Add the shrimp and cook, turning halfway through cooking, until pink and firm, about 3 minutes. Transfer to a plate, cover loosely, and set aside.

Add the remaining 3 tablespoons butter to the skillet and heat. Add the scallops and cook, turning halfway through cooking, until just opaque and firm, about 4 minutes. Remove from the heat. Return the shrimp to the skillet.

Drain the pasta well and return to the warm pot. Add the oil, basil, oregano, and red pepper flakes and toss. Add the shrimp and scallops and any butter in the skillet and toss again. Season with additional salt and the pepper.

Serve immediately in individual serving bowls. Using tongs, place the clams in their shells on top, ladle a spoonful of the clam juices over each serving, and sprinkle with the parsley.

Patti's Pointers: Timing is important with this version of this classic Italian favorite—the sauce should be done about the same time as the pasta.

Fabulous Fixin's

Awesome Asparagus

Makes **4 to 6** servings

2 pounds thin asparagus
2 tablespoons olive oil
2 garlic cloves, finely chopped
Grated zest of 1 lemon
Seasoned salt and freshly ground black pepper

Snap off and discard the tough parts of the asparagus stems. Cut the asparagus spears into 2-inch lengths.

In a large nonstick skillet, heat the oil over medium heat. Add the asparagus and garlic. Cover and cook, stirring occasionally, until the asparagus is barely tender, about 5 minutes. Stir in the lemon zest and season with salt and pepper. Serve hot.

Sautéed Broccoli Raab

This is one of those dishes that you are either going to love or hate. Believe me, it's going to be one or the other but nothing in between. Armstead is one of those people who love broccoli raab, which is why I learned to cook it. Like my live performances, this Italian vegetable packs a punch. When you bite into some broccoli raab, it just might bite you back. Just kidding. It tastes like regular broccoli, only it's stronger and more bitter. So come on, be brave; give this recipe a try.

Makes 4 to 6 servings

1½ pounds broccoli raab
3 tablespoons olive oil
2 garlic cloves, minced
Salt
Crushed red pepper flakes

Cut the stems crosswise into ½-inch-long pieces. Coarsely chop the leafy tops. Wash the broccoli raab well. Drain, but do not shake off the excess water.

In a large skillet, heat the oil over medium heat. Add the garlic and cook until softened, about 1 minute. Add the broccoli raab and cook, uncovered, stirring often, until the broccoli raab is tender, about 12 minutes. Season with salt and red pepper flakes to taste. Serve hot.

Patti's Pointers: Depending on where you buy it, broccoli raab is also called broccoli rabe, rape, or rapini. It looks like a leafy head of broccoli with small florets, but that's where the similarity ends. Because of its slightly bitter flavor, it goes great with pork, especially grilled chops or sausages. You can also toss the sautéed broccoli raab with hot pasta, douse it with olive oil, sprinkle it with Parmesan cheese, and call it dinner. (And a really good dinner, at that.)

Cabbage, Carrot, and Potato Skillet

This is a fantastic side dish for grilled sausage or pork chops.

Makes 6 to 8 servings

1 medium head green cabbage (about 2¼ pounds)
3 tablespoons butter
1 medium onion, chopped
2 medium carrots, cut into ½-inch dice
1 large red bell pepper, seeded and cut into ½-inch dice
2 large russet or Idaho potatoes, peeled and cut into
    1-inch cubes
2 cups water
Seasoned salt and crushed red pepper flakes
2 tablespoons chopped fresh cilantro or parsley, optional

Cut the cabbage into quarters. Cut off and discard the hard core from each wedge. Slice the cabbage into ½-inch-wide strips. Set aside.

In a deep 12-inch skillet, melt the butter over medium heat. Add the onion, carrots, and bell pepper. Cook, stirring often, until softened, about 5 minutes. Stir in the cabbage and potatoes. Add the water and season with salt and red pepper flakes to taste. Bring to a boil. Reduce the heat to medium-low and cover. Cook until the potatoes are tender and most of the liquid has evaporated, about 20 minutes. Transfer to a serving dish, and sprinkle with the cilantro, if desired. Serve hot.

Fierce Fried Corn

When I was a kid, I couldn't get enough of my father's fried corn. I loved it so much that when I was around 9 years old, I spilled a pot of boiling hot grease on myself trying to lift out a taste before anyone saw me.

I was upstairs playing when the sound and smell of fatback spitting and sizzling and simmering on the stove seemed to call my name. It was smelling so good, who could wait to taste it? Not me. By the time I reached the kitchen, my anticipation was running so high that when I stuck my fork in the pot, I turned the whole thing over on me.

Talk about pain. When that hot grease hit my neck, it felt like somebody had set me on fire. It burned my neck so badly, I had to be rushed to the hospital. To this day, I carry the scars.

Now, when I cook fried corn I use butter, not fatback. And I don't try to steal any before it's done.

Makes **4 to 6** servings

4 tablespoons (½ stick) butter
1 jalapeño, seeded and finely chopped, optional
4 cups fresh corn kernels (see Note, page 18)
Salt and freshly ground black pepper

In a large nonstick skillet, melt the butter over low heat. Add the jalapeño, if using. Add the corn, season with salt and pepper, and stir well. Cover and cook, stirring often, being very careful not to let the corn stick to the skillet, until the corn is heated through, 10 minutes. Serve hot.

Patti's Pointers: This is a recipe to save for when the corn is high on the stalk and inexpensive. Buy corn at a roadside stand or a farmer's market.

Corn Casserole

2 cups fresh corn kernels (see Note, page 18),
   thawed frozen corn, or drained canned corn
1 cup milk
2 large eggs, beaten
4 tablespoons (½ stick) butter, melted
1 tablespoon all-purpose flour
1 tablespoon sugar
½ teaspoon salt
⅛ teaspoon freshly ground black pepper

Preheat the oven to 325°F. Lightly butter an 8-inch square baking dish.

In a medium bowl, combine the corn, milk, eggs, butter, flour, sugar, salt, and pepper and mix well. Pour into the prepared dish.

Bake until a knife inserted in the center comes out clean, about 45 minutes. Let stand for 5 minutes. Serve hot.

Patti's Pointers: This is another recipe that you could make with frozen or canned corn, but is unbeatable with fresh kernels. You can make variations by stirring in ½ cup shredded sharp Cheddar cheese or 1 seeded and minced jalapeño, or both.

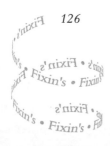

Screamin' Mean Greens

Makes 4 to 6 servings

5 pounds assorted greens (collard, kale, mustard,
    and turnip greens, in any combination), tough
    stems discarded
2 medium onions, chopped
¼ cup vegetable oil
2 jalapeños, seeded and minced, optional
One 1½-pound smoked turkey wing
Seasoned salt and freshly ground black pepper

Tear the greens into large pieces. Wash the greens well in a sink full of cold water. Lift the greens out of the sink and transfer to a large bowl, leaving the grit to fall to the bottom of the sink. (Be sure you get all the grit out of the greens. If necessary, wash again.) Do not drain the greens in a colander.

In a large pot, combine the onions, 2 cups water, oil, and jalapeños, if using. Bring to a boil over high heat. Gradually stir in the greens, allowing each batch to wilt before adding more greens. Bury the turkey wing in the greens. Season with salt and pepper to taste. Cover and reduce the heat to medium-low. Cook, stirring occasionally, just until the greens are tender, about 30 minutes. Do not overcook the greens or they will lose their color and fresh flavor. Remove the turkey wing. Discard the skin and bones, chop the turkey meat, and return to the pot. Using a slotted spoon, transfer the greens to a serving dish. Serve hot.

Patti's Pointers: Greens are a staple of Southern and African-American kitchens. Sometimes they are cooked to a fare-thee-well, but I think that diminishes their taste. Cook them just until tender and well seasoned with the turkey flavor, about 30 minutes.

Unforgettable Fried Eggplant

Makes **4 to 6** servings

Vegetable oil, for deep-frying
1 cup milk
2 large eggs
1¼ cups all-purpose flour
½ teaspoon salt, plus more to taste
¼ teaspoon freshly ground black pepper, plus more
   to taste
1 large eggplant (about 1¼ pounds)
2 tablespoons chopped fresh basil
2 tablespoons chopped fresh oregano
1 garlic clove, minced
Lemon wedges

Preheat the oven to 200°F. Line a baking sheet with paper towels and set aside.

Pour enough oil into a large, deep skillet to come halfway up the sides. Heat over high heat until very hot, but not smoking. (If you use an electric skillet, heat the oil to 365°F.)

In a medium bowl, beat the milk and eggs until combined. Add the flour, ½ teaspoon salt, and ¼ teaspoon pepper and whisk until smooth.

Slice the eggplant crosswise into ¼-inch-thick rounds. In batches without crowding, dip the eggplant into the batter, letting the excess batter drip back into the bowl. Fry until the underside is golden brown, about 2 minutes. Turn and fry until the other side is golden brown, about 2 minutes. Using a large skimmer or slotted pancake turner, transfer the eggplant to the paper towels. Keep warm in the oven while frying the remaining eggplant.

Transfer the eggplant to a serving platter. Season with salt and pepper. In a small bowl, combine the basil, oregano, and garlic. Sprinkle the eggplant with the basil mixture. Serve hot, with the lemon wedges.

Patti's Pointers: Don't chop the herbs until ready to serve—they can discolor if they stand around too long.

Mouthwatering Mushrooms

This is really elegant with shiitake mushrooms, but large button mushrooms, cut into quarters, are a good substitute.

Makes 4 servings

1 pound shiitake mushrooms
3 tablespoons olive oil
2 garlic cloves, minced
2 tablespoons chopped fresh cilantro, oregano, or
   parsley
Salt and crushed red pepper flakes

Rinse the mushrooms *quickly* to remove grit. Cut off and discard the tough stems.

In a large skillet, heat the oil over medium heat. Add the garlic and cook until fragrant, about 30 seconds. Add the mushrooms and cook, stirring often, until the mushrooms give off their juice and it evaporates, about 10 minutes. Stir in the cilantro and season with salt and red pepper flakes. Transfer to a serving dish and serve hot.

Cheesy Mushrooms: Transfer the mushrooms to a serving dish. Sprinkle with ½ cup shredded mozzarella cheese and cover loosely with aluminum foil. Let stand until the cheese melts, about 5 minutes. Sprinkle with the cilantro and serve immediately.

Okra, Corn, and Tomato Stew

Makes 4 to 6 servings

3 tablespoons unsalted butter
8 ounces okra, trimmed and sliced into ½-inch-
   thick rounds
4 cups fresh corn kernels (see Note, page 18)
1 medium onion, chopped
2 ripe beefsteak tomatoes, chopped
Seasoned salt and freshly ground black pepper

In a Dutch oven, melt the butter over medium heat. Add the okra, corn, onion, and tomatoes. Season with salt and pepper to taste. Bring to a simmer over medium heat, stirring often. Reduce the heat to medium-low and simmer until the okra is tender, about 35 minutes. Serve hot.

Shrimp with Okra, Corn, and Tomatoes: During the last 5 minutes of cooking, add 1½ pounds medium shrimp, peeled and deveined, and cook until the shrimp are pink and firm. Serve over hot cooked rice.

Home-Fried Potatoes

When I was 12 years old my parents separated. Though their split was violent and ugly, to my parents' credit, they worked it out so my father could see my sisters and me as often as possible. For the first two years after the separation, Daddy would come by two, sometimes three, times a week. On weekends, he would come over early in the morning just to cook our breakfast.

You want to know the best thing about those breakfasts? The fact that my daddy was home cooking them for us just the way he used to before The Awful Night. The night that turned my world upside down. The night Chubby discovered the apartment Daddy was keeping downtown with another woman. The night she pulled a knife on him and told him if he didn't leave for good, she'd use it.

On weekends, it was almost as if The Awful Night never happened. During those early-morning breakfasts, I could pretend it didn't. Of course, having Daddy home made everything taste extra special. Especially his homefries. Like his fried corn, Daddy's homefries were world-class. When the potatoes were just about done, he would pour some water in the pan, put a top on it, and let them steam so they would melt in your mouth. To this day, that's how I cook mine.

In a funny way, those homefries made my parents' separation bearable. It still hurt me deeply, but when I was sitting at the kitchen table eating breakfast with Daddy, I felt safe again—like, even if things weren't the same, they were going to be all right. During those early-morning breakfasts, the bond between Daddy and me strengthened itself on homefries and love.

It's because of those breakfasts that, more than forty years later, I always give the same answer when people see me grocery shopping and ask, "Patti, you cooking some soul food tonight?"

"I sure am, Sugar," I always say. It doesn't matter what I'm cooking—sautéed salmon or shrimp fried rice. Soul food, it seems to me, is food that soothes the soul. I learned that from my daddy's homefries.

¼ cup olive oil
1½ pounds red-skinned potatoes, peeled and cut
    into ¼-inch-thick rounds
1 medium onion, sliced into ⅛-inch-thick half-
    moons
½ cup water
Seasoned salt and freshly ground black pepper

In a large nonstick skillet, heat the oil over medium-high heat. Spread the potatoes in the skillet, then top with the onion. Cook until most of the potatoes on the bottom of the skillet have browned, about 5 minutes. Turn the potatoes and onions. Cook until the new layer of potatoes on the bottom has browned, about 5 minutes. Turn again, and pour the water over the potatoes. Reduce the heat to medium and cover tightly. Cook, stirring occasionally, until the potatoes are well browned and tender and the water has evaporated, about 10 minutes. (If desired, uncover and cook until the potatoes crisp, about 5 minutes.) Season with salt and pepper to taste. Serve hot.

Patti's Pointers: Use red-skinned potatoes to make the best homefries—they won't crumble apart like the all-purpose russet variety.

Better-Than-Mom's Mashed Potatoes

Makes **4 to 6** servings

3 pounds russet or Idaho baking potatoes
½ cup half-and-half
6 tablespoons (¾ stick) unsalted butter, softened
Salt and freshly ground black pepper

Peel the potatoes and cut into 1-inch chunks. Place in a large pot and add enough lightly salted water to cover the potatoes by 1 inch. Cover and bring to a boil over high heat. Reduce the heat to medium. Cook, covered, until the potatoes are tender, 15 to 20 minutes. Drain well.

Return the potatoes to the pot. Using a potato masher or electric hand mixer, gradually adding the half-and-half and butter, mash the potatoes until smooth and fluffy. Season with salt and pepper to taste. Transfer to a serving dish and serve immediately.

Perfectly Steamed Rice

Makes **4 to 6** servings

3 cups water
1½ cups long-grain rice
1 tablespoon butter
1 teaspoon salt
¼ teaspoon freshly ground black pepper

In a medium saucepan, bring the water, rice, butter, salt, and pepper to a boil over high heat. Reduce the heat to low and cover tightly. Simmer until the liquid is absorbed and the rice is tender, about 20 minutes. Remove from the heat and let stand, covered, for 5 minutes. Fluff the rice with a fork and serve hot.

Yellow Rice: Stir ¼ teaspoon crushed saffron threads or ½ teaspoon ground turmeric into the water.

Patti's Pointers: Maybe the most important part about cooking rice is picking the right pot. It should be heavy-bottomed with a tight-fitting lid. Also, it should be just big enough to comfortably hold the cooked rice. Raw rice triples in size when cooked, so this recipe makes about 4½ cups. A 1½-quart saucepan is perfect.

Armstead's Curried Rice and Beans

Here's a dish that's tasty, well seasoned, quick to make, and very versatile. Serve it as a side dish or even as a vegetarian main course. You can make it more substantial by adding bite-sized pieces of cooked ham or roast pork to the okra mixture. Or, if you're not an okra fan, substitute green beans. If you don't care for kidney beans, try garbanzos. Make it any way you want—Armstead won't mind.

Curry powders, especially when purchased from health food or spice stores, vary in spiciness. If you want a good, solid brand with a middle-of-the-road heat level, use Madras-style curry powder, available in small tins at the supermarket.

My niece Stephanie and her father, Jack, enjoying some snacks while they wait for Armstead (at stove) to finish cooking his world-famous curried rice and beans.

2 cups water
1 cup long-grain rice
2 vegetable bouillon cubes, crumbled
2 teaspoons curry powder
¼ teaspoon ground turmeric
¼ teaspoon salt
1 tablespoon vegetable oil
2 green onions, white and green parts, chopped
2 garlic cloves, minced
One 10-ounce package thawed frozen cut okra
One 15½-ounce can kidney beans, drained and
    rinsed

In a medium saucepan, bring the water, rice, bouillon cubes, curry powder, turmeric, and salt to a boil over high heat. Reduce the heat to low and cover tightly. Cook until the rice is tender and absorbs the liquid, about 18 minutes.

Meanwhile, in a large skillet, heat the oil over medium heat. Add the green onions and garlic and cook, stirring occasionally, until softened, about 2 minutes. Stir in the okra and kidney beans and bring to a simmer.

Add the rice mixture and stir just until combined. Serve immediately.

Spectacular Spinach

2 pounds spinach, tough stems discarded
2 tablespoons olive oil
2 garlic cloves, finely chopped
Seasoned salt and freshly ground black pepper

Wash the spinach well in a sink of cold water. Lift the spinach out of the water and transfer to a large bowl, leaving the grit to fall to the bottom of the sink. Do not drain the spinach in a colander.

In a Dutch oven, heat the olive oil over medium-high heat. Add the garlic. In batches, add the spinach with the water clinging to its leaves, stirring until it wilts before adding more, and season with salt and pepper to taste. Cook, uncovered, stirring often, just until the spinach is tender, about 5 minutes. Serve hot.

Patti's Pointers: If you can find tender spinach in bunches, you'll really love this spinach. No matter what, be sure you rinse the spinach well to remove every single last bit of tiny grit.

String Beans à La Bella

This dish is very special to me because it was my sister Barbara's favorite. Just the smell of it takes me back to her wedding day. And oh what a day it was! We had the best food, the best company, the best time. And I will be forever grateful for that perfect day because, more than any other affair I've hosted, I needed Barbara's wedding to be special. I needed it to fulfill all her expectations.

You see, not long before Barbara wed, she learned she had colon cancer. "Just let me know what you need," I said when she told me about the diagnosis. "Anything you want, I'll do it."

What Barbara wanted was a fairy-tale wedding. Despite the diagnosis, she and her fiancé decided to go forward with the marriage because, as Barbara said to me: "We can't control the future, Patsy. But we can make the most of every moment we're given."

You can see why I was so determined to make my sister's wedding day everything she had always dreamed of and more. Of course, that meant I couldn't entrust Barbara's favorite

Friends 'til the end: Maudie Hurd (left) and Llona Gullette stayed up all night with me helping cook Barbara's favorite dishes for her 200 wedding guests.

dishes to some caterer. Especially my String Beans à La Bella. But, I had to be practical. With 200 confirmed guests, I needed help. And I needed it bad.

Luckily, two dear friends—women from the old neighborhood I've known my whole life—offered their assistance. And since I knew how well they cooked, I gladly accepted. The night before Barbara's wedding, Miss Maudie, Llona

Fixin's • Fixin's • Fixin's
Fixin's • Fixin's
Fixin's • Fixin's • Fixin's

Gullette, and I cooked until the wee hours of the morning. And the food, like the day, turned out perfect.

Two years later, Barbara died. After all these years, her words—"We can't control the future, Patsy. But we can make the most of every moment we're given"—still echo in my dreams. For the repast, Llona and Miss Maudie helped me re-create Barbara's wedding day menu. Both understood why I had to make the String Beans à La Bella myself.

The next time you're celebrating something special, whether it's a formal dinner or a casual cookout, do me a favor. Cook up a huge pot of String Beans à La Bella, the biggest one you can find. For those few hours, let go of the past and take your eyes off the future. Whatever you're celebrating—a wedding, a graduation, a birthday, a baptism—really cherish it, relish it, live completely in the moment. Barbara would like that. And so would I.

Makes 6 to 8 servings

1 medium Vidalia or other white onion, chopped
One 14½-ounce can chopped tomatoes, with juice
One 6-ounce can tomato paste
¾ cup water
1 tablespoon olive oil
1 tablespoon chopped fresh oregano or 1½ teaspoons dried
1 garlic clove, chopped
1 pound string beans, trimmed, cut into 2-inch lengths
Seasoned salt
Freshly ground black pepper
Crushed red pepper flakes
½ cup (2 ounces) shredded mozzarella cheese
½ cup (2 ounces) shredded provolone cheese

In a Dutch oven, combine the onion, tomatoes with their juice, tomato paste, water, olive oil, oregano, and garlic; stir well to dissolve the tomato paste. Add the string beans and season to taste with salt, black pepper, and red pepper flakes. Bring to a boil over medium heat. Cover and cook until the beans are very tender and are swimming in a thick tomato sauce, about 30 minutes. (The sauce should remind you of spaghetti sauce.)

Remove the Dutch oven from the heat. Sprinkle the cheese over the beans and replace the cover. Let stand until the cheese melts, about 5 minutes. (Or, layer the string beans and cheese in a serving dish, cover with aluminum foil, and let stand until the cheese melts, about 5 minutes.) Serve immediately.

Patti's Pointers: There are two ways to cook green beans—quickly cooked until crisp-tender or slowly cooked until smothered. Here, I smother them in an oregano-scented tomato sauce, then melt some Italian cheese into them for extra goodness.

My beloved sister Barbara.

Sumptuous String Beans

Makes **4 to 6** servings

2 tablespoons olive oil
1 medium onion, finely chopped
1 garlic clove, finely chopped
1 pound string beans, trimmed, cut into 2-inch
    lengths
Seasoned salt and freshly ground black pepper

In a large nonstick skillet, heat the oil over medium heat. Add the onion and garlic and cook until softened, about 3 minutes. Add the string beans and cover. Cook, stirring occasionally, until the green beans are crisp-tender, about 6 minutes. Season to taste with salt and pepper. Serve hot.

Sautéed Summer Squash with Basil

Any yellow summer squash, like crookneck or golden zucchini, will work here. It's good with green zucchini, too.

Makes 4 to 6 servings

2 pounds yellow squash
1 tablespoon butter
1 tablespoon olive oil
1 medium onion, chopped
2 garlic cloves, finely chopped
1 large ripe tomato, cut into ½-inch dice
2 tablespoons chopped fresh basil
Seasoned salt and freshly ground black pepper

Rinse the squash well. Cut crosswise into ¼-inch-thick rounds and set aside.

In a large skillet, heat the butter and olive oil over medium heat. Add the squash, onion, and garlic. Cook, uncovered, stirring often, until tender, about 10 minutes. Add the tomato and basil and cook, stirring occasionally, until the tomato is heated through, about 3 minutes. Season to taste with salt and pepper. Serve hot.

Chubby's Candied Sweet Potatoes

Makes 6 to 8 servings

8 medium orange-fleshed sweet potatoes, scrubbed
    but unpeeled (4 pounds)
½ cup packed light brown sugar
½ cup granulated sugar
¾ cup chopped pecans
½ teaspoon ground cinnamon
½ teaspoon ground nutmeg
¼ teaspoon ground ginger
8 tablespoons (1 stick) unsalted butter, softened
½ cup boiling water

Preheat the oven to 325°F. Lightly butter a 9 × 13-inch baking dish.

Bring a large pot of lightly salted water to a boil over high heat. Add the sweet potatoes. Cook until tender, about 25 minutes. Drain. Rinse under cold running water until cool enough to handle. Peel the sweet potatoes.

In a medium bowl, combine the sugars, pecans, cinnamon, nutmeg, and ginger. Slicing the sweet potatoes into ½-inch-thick rounds as you go, layer about one-third of the sweet potatoes in the prepared baking dish. Sprinkle with one-third of the sugar/pecan mixture and dot with one-third (a scant 3 tablespoons) of the butter. Repeat with another layer of sweet potatoes, half of the remaining sugar/pecan mixture, and another scant 3 tablespoons of butter. Top with the final layer of potatoes, the remaining sugar/pecan mixture, and the remaining butter. Pour the boiling water into the dish, around the sweet potatoes, not over them.

Bake, basting occasionally with the syrup that forms in the dish, until the sweet potatoes are glazed, about 45 minutes. Let stand 5 minutes. Serve hot.

Patti's Pointers: Use good old orange-fleshed sweet potatoes, sometimes called Louisiana yams. I have to make the distinction because many supermarkets now carry the yellow-fleshed "true" sweet potatoes *(batatas),* which are drier than the Southern variety.

Mashed Sweet Potatoes

Good for a Sunday supper of baked ham and macaroni and cheese.

Makes **4 to 6** servings

5 medium orange-fleshed sweet potatoes, scrubbed
    but unpeeled (3 pounds)
4 tablespoons (½ stick) unsalted butter, softened
¼ cup sugar
¼ teaspoon ground cinnamon
¼ cup heavy cream
Grated zest of 1 orange or lemon, optional

Bring a large pot of lightly salted water to a boil over high heat. Add the sweet potatoes. Cook until tender, about 25 minutes. Drain. Rinse under cold running water until cool enough to handle. Peel the sweet potatoes and return to the warm pot.

Add the butter, sugar, and cinnamon. Mash with a potato masher or handheld electric mixer until smooth. Stir in the cream. Transfer to a serving dish. If desired, sprinkle with the orange zest. Serve hot.

Quick 'n' Easy Baked Beans

Makes **8 to 10** servings

Five 16-ounce cans baked beans, drained
½ cup maple-flavored pancake syrup
½ cup ketchup
3 tablespoons prepared yellow mustard
1½ tablespoons light brown sugar
1½ tablespoons prepared horseradish
1½ teaspoons dry mustard

Preheat the oven to 375°F. Lightly grease a deep 2½-quart casserole dish.

In the prepared casserole, mix the beans, syrup, ketchup, yellow mustard, brown sugar, horseradish, and dry mustard until well combined.

Bake, uncovered, stirring occasionally, until bubbling, about 40 minutes. Serve hot.

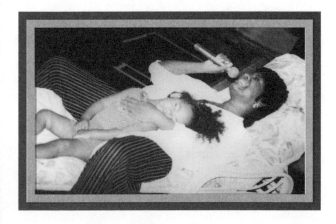

Singing my friend Taylor to sleep after an all-day cook-out. I think all the food the child ate knocked her out.

147

Black-Eyed Peas with Smoked Turkey Wings

Makes **6 to 8** servings

1 pound dried black-eyed peas
Two 1½-pound smoked turkey wings
2 medium onions, chopped
1 jalapeño, seeded and minced, optional
Seasoned salt and freshly ground black pepper

Rinse the black-eyed peas well, sorting through them to remove any small stones. Place in a Dutch oven and add enough cold water to cover by 2 inches. Cover and let stand for 30 minutes. Drain the peas, rinse with cold water, and return to the pot.

Add the turkey wings, onions, and jalapeño, if desired. Add just enough cold water to cover the peas. Bring to a boil over high heat. Reduce the heat to low. Simmer, uncovered, adding boiling water if needed to keep the peas covered, until the peas are tender and the cooking liquid has thickened, about 45 minutes.

Remove the turkey wings. Discard the skin and bones. Chop the meat and stir back into the pot. Season with salt and pepper to taste. Serve hot.

Note: *You can substitute 2 tablespoons instant ham seasoning (such as Goya) for the turkey wings.*

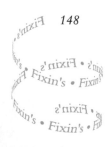

Red Beans and Rice

Here's a dish I love to spice up with hot sauce, but only if it lives up to its name: *hot*. I don't have any use for that mild, sissy stuff. On the subject of hot sauce, I have a simple philosophy: mo' hotta, mo' betta. When Miss Patti uses hot drops, they have to be the real deal. I'm talking ring-of-fire, turbo-charged, sinus-busting hot! Thanks to my fans, who bring me bottles and bottles of the stuff whenever I tour, I have had the chance to sample hot sauces from all over the world: China's Amoy Chinesis Wurzsauce Chili Sauce (don't ask me to pronounce it), Jamaica's Hell Fire Hot Pepper Concentrate (flavorsome), Trinidad's Calypso Kitchen (seriously spicy), and Canada's Caribbean Gourmet Triple Barn Burner Super Hot Sauce (yummy!). And last, but not least, from right here at home, Dave's Gourmet Insanity Sauce (suffice it to say that it's made with capsicum oleoresin, a pepper extract that's an ingredient in pepper spray, the assault weapon in a can).

For years, I've been working on my top secret recipe for the ultimate hot sauce. I haven't perfected it yet, but it's just a matter of time!

This recipe is so good, however, if you aren't a devout chile head like me, you can leave out the hot drops and it will still light your fire.

Makes **6 servings**

1 pound dried red beans
10 bacon strips (see Patti's Pointers)
1 large onion, chopped
1 medium green bell pepper, seeded and chopped
2 medium celery ribs, chopped
3 garlic cloves, chopped
1 pound andouille, hot links, or kielbasa sausage, cut
   into ½-inch-thick rounds
2 tablespoons chopped fresh thyme
Seasoned salt and freshly ground black pepper
Hot red pepper sauce
Perfectly Steamed Rice (page 135)

The night before cooking, rinse the beans and sort through them for little stones. Place the beans in a large bowl and add enough cold water to cover by 3 inches. Let stand for 4 hours or up to overnight, if you wish. (Or, place the rinsed beans in a Dutch oven, add enough cold water to cover by 3 inches, and bring to a boil over high heat. Boil for 1 minute. Remove from the heat, cover tightly, and let stand for 1 hour.) Drain.

Place the beans in a Dutch oven and add enough fresh cold water to just cover the beans. Cover tightly and bring to a boil over high heat. Reduce the heat to medium–low, and simmer, covered, for 45 minutes. Add more hot water to the beans to keep them covered, if needed.

Meanwhile, in a large skillet, cook the bacon over medium-high heat until crisp and brown, about 5 minutes. Transfer the bacon to paper towels to drain. When cooled, crumble the bacon and set aside. Pour off all but 3 tablespoons of the bacon fat in the skillet.

Add the onion, green pepper, celery, and garlic to the skillet and cook over medium heat, stirring occasionally, until softened, about 8 minutes.

After the beans have cooked for 45 minutes, stir in the cooked vegetables, crumbled bacon, sausage, thyme, and salt and pepper to taste. Cook, uncovered, stirring often, until the beans are tender and the cooking liquid has formed a thick sauce, about 30 minutes. Season well with hot pepper sauce.

To serve, spoon the rice into individual bowls, and ladle the red beans over the rice.

Patti's Pointers: If desired, substitute a smoked turkey wing for the bacon. Substitute 3 tablespoons of vegetable oil for the bacon drippings to sauté the vegetables. Add one 1½-pound smoked turkey wing to the beans during the 45 minutes of cooking. Discard the skin and bones, chop the turkey meat, and return to the beans.

Don't-Block-the-Blessing Dressing

I make my stuffing on top of the stove in a skillet, not in the oven. It's just the way I prefer it—you can use it to stuff your bird, if you like. This makes enough for a roasting chicken or small turkey, up to 12 pounds. If you want enough for a holiday-sized crowd, make a double batch, dividing the stuffing between two large skillets.

The stuffing is best if you add some chicken or turkey drippings from the roasting pan to the butter while cooking the vegetables. You can do this after the bird comes out of the oven—a turkey should stand for about 30 minutes before carving, anyway—or siphon off the drippings as they accumulate during roasting with a bulb baster.

I can't tell you how moist to make your dressing, so add enough broth to your liking. It shouldn't be soggy, but it shouldn't be dry, either. The kind of bread is up to you, too. I use a soft sandwich bread (like Wonder Bread), but you might like a firmer loaf (like Pepperidge Farm). If you wish, cut the bread into cubes and let it stand out overnight to dry out before using.

Makes 6 to 8 servings

12 tablespoons (1½ sticks) butter, substituting some
    turkey or chicken drippings for an equal amount of
    butter, if desired
1 large onion, chopped
3 medium celery ribs, chopped
1 medium green pepper, seeded and chopped
2 jalapeños, seeded and finely chopped, optional
3 tablespoons chopped fresh oregano (or 3 tablespoons
    chopped fresh parsley and 1 teaspoon dried oregano)
1 tablespoon poultry seasoning
1 teaspoon celery seed
1 pound white sandwich bread, cut into pieces about
    ½ inch square
1½ cups turkey or chicken broth, approximately
Seasoned salt and freshly ground black pepper

In a deep, 12-inch nonstick skillet, heat 4 tablespoons of the butter over medium-high heat. Add the onion, celery, green pepper, and jalapeños, if using. Cook, uncovered, stirring often, until the vegetables are tender, about 12 minutes. Add the oregano, poultry seasoning, and celery seed. Add the remaining 8 tablespoons butter and melt.

    In a large bowl, toss the bread with 1 cup of the broth to lightly moisten the bread. Add to the skillet, mixing well, adding more broth to reach the desired moistness. Reduce the heat to very low and cover. Cook, stirring occasionally, until the dressing is heated through, about 10 minutes. Season to taste with salt and pepper.

Over-the-Rainbow Macaroni and Cheese

I don't know who turned Elton John on to soul music but I do know who turned him on to soul food. Me. At least I'm pretty sure it was me. Back in the sixties, when Patti LaBelle and the Bluebelles was touring London, the British band, Bluesology, played backup to us. Elton, or Reggie Dwight as he was known in those days, was the band's piano player, and he played like no other White boy I have ever heard.

For some reason, Reggie thought he could play cards like he could play keyboards. After our shows, he'd come back to our flat and challenge me to a game of tonk. No matter how many times I beat him—and I beat him all the time—Reggie wouldn't quit until I'd won all his money.

"Just one more game, Patti," he would plead, "and I'll win back all my pounds."

Of course, the only thing he ever won was my sympathy. Not enough to give the money back, of course. But sufficient to make me cook enough food to make sure the kid wouldn't go hungry before payday. After I stashed Reggie's cash, I prepared him a savory, spicy, soul food feast: smothered cabbage, red beans and rice, fried chicken and potato salad—you name it, I cooked it.

It was impossible to eat everything—although Reggie tried. But it was my macaroni and cheese that he loved the most. As you can see from the recipe, I make it with five different kinds of cheese, and that's how many times Reggie went back for more.

He wanted recipes for everything. But, since I kept them top secret until I wrote this book, he had to settle for the food sans the instructions on how to prepare it. I always sent Reg home with enough to feed an army, though. We're talking containers of food. Come to think of it, Boyfriend never did return any of my Tupperware. Now that might not be a big deal to most people, but to me it's a high crime.

Ask anyone who knows me. It's not rational I know, but I have a serious thing about my plastic containers. I will give you the food off my stove and shirt off my back, but not my Tupperware! That I want back!

And I don't mean a month or two later. People think I'm kidding when I tell them they have to return it within a week, but I'm not. Just ask my niece Stayce. A month after I'd sent her home with several containers full of food, she still hadn't brought them back. I called her up and had a hissy fit. I must have fussed at Stayce a good ten minutes before I realized she was crying.

"But, Aunt Patsy," she said, sobbing, "I didn't think you were serious."

"I'm sorry I made you cry, Baby," I said, "but bring me my containers by the weekend."

So, Reggie, I mean Elton, if you're reading this, I love you dearly, Rocket Man. But I want my Tupperware back!! 🎼

Makes 4 to 6 servings

1 tablespoon vegetable oil
1 pound elbow macaroni
8 tablespoons (1 stick) plus 1 tablespoon butter
½ cup (2 ounces) shredded Muenster cheese
½ cup (2 ounces) shredded mild Cheddar cheese
½ cup (2 ounces) shredded sharp Cheddar cheese
½ cup (2 ounces) shredded Monterey Jack
2 cups half-and-half
1 cup (8 ounces) Velveeta, cut into small cubes
2 large eggs, lightly beaten
¼ teaspoon seasoned salt
⅛ teaspoon freshly ground black pepper

Preheat the oven to 350°F. Lightly butter a deep 2½-quart casserole.

Bring a large pot of salted water to a boil over high heat. Add the oil, then the elbow macaroni, and cook until the macaroni is just tender, about 7 minutes. Do not overcook. Drain well. Return to the cooking pot.

In a small saucepan, melt 8 tablespoons of the butter. Stir into the macaroni. In a large bowl, mix the Muenster, mild and sharp Cheddar, and Monterey Jack cheeses. To the macaroni, add the half-and-half, 1½ cups of the shredded cheese, the cubed Velveeta, and the eggs. Season with the salt and pepper. Transfer to the buttered casserole. Sprinkle with the remaining ½ cup of shredded cheese and dot with the remaining 1 tablespoon of butter.

Bake until it's bubbling around the edges, about 35 minutes. Serve hot.

Patti's Pointers: Ask anyone who makes incredible macaroni and cheese for his or her recipe, and I bet you that Velveeta will be in there. But my recipe doesn't stop there. To make my special macaroni and cheese, I also use Muenster, mild and sharp Cheddar, and Monterey Jack cheeses, each one adding its own flavor and melting consistency. If you don't want to use all five cheeses, you can get away with just the Velveeta and sharp Cheddar—it won't be over the rainbow, but it will be pretty good. And, on special occasions, I sometimes add an extra stick of butter, in which instance, the macaroni goes over the moon! If you use two sticks of butter, substitute milk for the half-and-half.

To-Die-For Desserts and
Breads

Aunt Mary's Philadelphia Buttercake

I wanted them to feel Mary's presence, their linkage to her spirit, to her love, to all our loved ones who weren't with us at the table but were with us in our hearts. It was Christmas 1996 and my family was still in mourning. Several weeks earlier, we had lost Armstead's sister, Mary, when she had a massive heart attack and died in her sleep.

No one came out and said so, but I knew everyone was dreading Christmas dinner. We were all going to have to operate on automatic pilot, acting as if things were as they always were, as if nothing had changed when everything had.

For as long as any of us could remember, it was Mary who hosted our holiday meals. The time, the thought, and the tender loving care she put into preparing them always made us feel like a family in the truest sense of the word. Everything about Mary's Christmas dinners—from the dishes to the decorations—was so beautiful that they had a kind of magical, it's-a-wonderful-life quality to them. As a result, they connected us not only to each other, but to a sacred family tradition that affirmed who we were and where we belonged. And so when Mary died the month before Christmas, it cracked something whole in our holiday—and in our hearts.

I knew I couldn't eliminate the pain we all were feeling but, in an effort to ease it, I'd gone all out to try and make the day special. For two days, I'd done nothing but cook—not just turkey with all the trimmings but also leg of lamb, ham, lobster, shrimp, salmon, and a mountain of desserts, including this family favorite, Mary's specialty. I'd even had the house professionally decorated—everywhere you looked there were garlands, wreaths, angels, poinsettias, fresh flowers, and fragrant candles—in the hope that its beauty would lift our spirits.

But no one was merry without Mary. As I watched my family faking smiles and struggling to get through the day, I thought of all the things, both real and restorative, that I could say to them about Mary's death. I thought about how

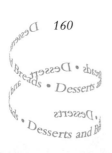

much family meant to Mary and the legacy she had left us: the love-getting, spirit-lifting, joy-giving Christmas dinners that she, more than anyone, would want us, her family, to keep alive. I thought about what Mary would say to us—especially to her mother and her daughter and her grandbabies—if she could be here with us one last Christmas.

That's what I was thinking when, before we sat down to eat, I asked everyone to gather in the kitchen where I wanted to bless the meal. I can't recall the specifics of what I said; I just remember small details—asking everyone to hold hands, closing my eyes and asking God to bless me with the right words, then saying what was in my heart.

I talked about my memories of Christmas past: the food, the festivities, the sights, the smells, the sounds. I remembered the very first Christmas I'd tasted Mary's buttercake, how I wanted to eat the whole thing—piece by piece, bite by bite—right then and there.

And little by little, memory and history came together to help me say a lot of things I'd been feeling but never

Aunt Mary and Zuri hanging out together. The way he's holding on to that homemade cookie she gave him, you'd think it was made of gold!

knew how to say: how, at age 81, Anna Edwards—Mary's mother, my mother-in-law, and Armstead's family matriarch—had buried not one, not two, but *three* children. How just watching her—her courage, her quiet strength, her refusal to allow her grief to incapacitate her—had taught me more about loss and how to deal with it than words could ever say.

I talked about how, unlike me, my mother-in-law didn't get to go on stage and scream and cry and sing out her pain. About how for years, I could never

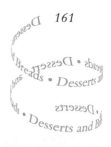

understand how she bore it. And then it came to me. Finally, I told my family, I thought I understood what kept my mother-in-law going in the face of unimaginable loss and unholy pain. It was what she knew deep inside her—in her heart, in her soul, in the marrow of her bones: *People die but love doesn't.* Like the generations of a family, love goes on and on. And, even when we lose someone before we're ready, we must, too.

It wasn't until I told my relatives I was writing this cookbook and I wanted to include Mary's buttercake that I learned how they felt about that day, that dinner, that prayer. And what they told me has helped me to make a small payment on an enormous debt I owe to Mary. And to my soul's account.

"Your words touched everyone in the room, both young and old," Mary's niece, Fahja, told me. "It transformed the day."

"You will never know how much what you did that first Christmas without Mom meant to us," Mary's daughter, Stephanie, said. "I will always remember it as something special, precious, and beautiful."

As we will remember Mary. And her unforgettable buttercake.

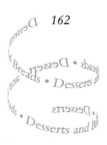

CAKE

1 medium russet or Idaho potato, peeled and cut
    into ¾-inch cubes (about 9 ounces)
One ¼-ounce package active dry yeast
½ cup sugar
2 tablespoons butter, at room temperature
1 large egg, at room temperature
½ teaspoon salt
2½ cups unbleached all-purpose flour,
    approximately

TOPPING

6 tablespoons (¾ stick) butter, at room temperature
¾ cup sugar
1 large egg, at room temperature
¼ cup unbleached all-purpose flour
3 tablespoons milk

To make the cake: Place the potato in a medium saucepan and add enough un-salted water to cover by 1 inch. Bring to a boil over high heat. Reduce the heat to medium-low and cook until the potato is very tender, about 15 minutes. Drain in a sieve (wire strainer), reserving ½ cup plus 2 tablespoons of the potato cooking liquid. Press the potato through the sieve into a medium bowl—the potatoes should be absolutely lump-free. Stir in 6 tablespoons of the potato water; set aside. Let the mashed potato mixture and remaining 4 tablespoons potato water stand, stirring occasionally, until tepid (100° to 110°F), about 20 minutes.

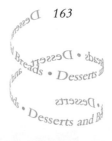

163

In a small bowl, sprinkle the yeast over the tepid 4 tablespoons potato water. Let stand for 5 minutes, then stir to dissolve the yeast.

In a large bowl, using an electric mixer at high speed, beat the sugar and butter until well combined and crumbly, about 1 minute. Beat in the egg, salt, potato mixture, and the dissolved yeast. With the mixer on low speed, gradually beat in 1 cup of the flour. Using a wooden spoon, gradually stir in another 1 cup of the flour to make a soft, sticky dough. Turn out the dough onto a floured work surface.

Knead the dough, adding more flour as needed, until smooth and shiny, about 10 minutes. The dough should be soft and slightly sticky—add just enough flour to keep the dough from sticking to the work surface. Gather the dough up into a ball. Place in a well-buttered medium bowl, and turn to coat the dough with butter. Cover with plastic wrap and let stand in a warm, draft-free place until doubled in volume (your finger will leave an impression in the dough), about 1 hour.

Lightly butter a 13 × 9-inch baking pan. Punch down the dough and knead briefly to expel the air. Stretch and pull the dough to fit into the prepared pan, being sure to fill the corners. Cover with plastic wrap and let stand until puffed almost double, about 30 minutes. (After 5 minutes, if the dough shrinks from the corners, stretch the dough again.)

Preheat the oven to 350°F. To make the topping: Using an electric mixer at high speed, beat the butter and sugar until light in color and texture, about 2 minutes. Beat in the egg, then the flour. Beat in the milk to give the mixture a frosting-like consistency. Spread evenly over the top of the dough.

Bake until the topping is golden brown, about 40 minutes. Cool in the pan on a wire cake rack for 30 minutes. Serve warm, or cool completely and serve at room temperature.

Patti's Pointers: To some cooks, a butter cake would be a frosted yellow layer cake. But this is "buttercake," and to Aunt Mary, and many other Philadelphians, that means a sweet yeast cake with a crackled butter-rich topping. (If you want more of a good thing, double the topping recipe.)

Potatoes, and their cooking water, give the dough its moist, chewy texture. The potatoes and cooking water must be tepid before they are mixed with the yeast, because hot ingredients would kill the yeast. Tepid means 100° to 110°F, so use a thermometer if you aren't sure.

Because of the sugar, egg, and butter, the dough will feel soft and sticky during kneading—that's fine! Knead in just enough flour to keep the dough from sticking to the work surface. If you add too much flour, the cake will be heavy.

Heavenly Carrot Cake with
Cream Cheese Frosting

Many carrot cakes call for grated carrots, but shredding vegetables isn't every-one's favorite kitchen chore. This cake gets its flavor from carrot baby food, and it works! The next time you need to bring a cake to a picnic, make this one—it's easy to transport right in its pan. My family likes lots of icing. If you want a moderate amount of frosting, just halve the recipe.

Makes 15 servings

CAKE

2½ cups all-purpose flour
2 teaspoons baking soda
½ teaspoon ground cinnamon
⅛ teaspoon ground allspice
½ teaspoon salt
2 cups sugar
1 cup vegetable oil
2 large eggs, at room temperature
2 teaspoons vanilla extract
Four 4-ounce jars carrot baby food (1½ cups)
One 8-ounce can crushed pineapple, well drained
¾ cup (3 ounces) chopped walnuts
½ cup raisins

FROSTING

8 ounces cream cheese, at room temperature
4 tablespoons (½ stick) butter, at room temperature
1 tablespoon half-and-half or milk
½ teaspoon almond extract
½ teaspoon vanilla extract
4 cups confectioners' sugar (1 pound)

15 walnut halves, optional

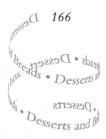

To make the cake: Preheat the oven to 350°F. Lightly butter and flour a 13 × 9-inch baking pan, tapping out the excess flour. Sift the flour, baking soda, cinnamon, allspice, and salt together and set aside.

In a large bowl, using an electric mixer at high speed, beat the sugar, oil, eggs, and vanilla until well combined, about 1 minute. Mix in the carrot baby food. With the mixer on low speed, beat in the flour mixture, scraping down the sides of the bowl as needed, and mix until smooth. Using a wooden spoon, stir in the pineapple, chopped walnuts, and raisins. Spread evenly in the prepared pan.

Bake until the top springs back when pressed lightly in the center, about 1 hour. Cool completely in the pan on a wire cake rack.

To make the frosting: In a medium bowl, using an electric mixer at medium speed, beat the cream cheese, butter, half-and-half, and almond and vanilla extracts until smooth, scraping down the sides of the bowl with a rubber spatula. With the mixer on low speed, gradually beat in the confectioners' sugar.

Spread the frosting over the top of the cake. Cut into 15 pieces. If desired, garnish each piece of cake with a walnut half.

Chocolate Cake with Mocha Madness Frosting

If you are a frosting lover, this is the recipe for you. It makes almost too much frosting, but who cares?

Makes 8 servings

CAKE LAYERS

1¾ cups all-purpose flour
½ cup unsweetened cocoa powder, such as
   Hershey's
1 teaspoon baking soda
½ teaspoon salt
8 tablespoons (1 stick) butter, softened
¾ cup packed light brown sugar
½ cup granulated sugar
2 large eggs, at room temperature
1 teaspoon vanilla extract
1 cup buttermilk

FROSTING

⅓ cup milk
¼ cup chocolate syrup
2 teaspoons instant coffee dissolved in 1 tablespoon
   boiling water
1 teaspoon vanilla extract
4 cups confectioners' sugar
¾ cup unsweetened cocoa powder, such as
   Hershey's
8 tablespoons (1 stick) butter, at room temperature

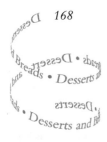

To make the cake layers: Preheat the oven to 350°F. Lightly butter and flour two 8-inch round cake pans, tapping out the excess flour. Sift the flour, cocoa, baking soda, and salt into a medium bowl and set aside.

In a large bowl, using an electric mixer at high speed, beat the butter until creamy, about 1 minute. Add the brown and granulated sugars and beat until light and fluffy, about 2 minutes. One at a time, beat in the eggs, then the vanilla. Reduce the mixer speed to low. In three additions, beat in the flour/cocoa mixture, alternating with the buttermilk, scraping the bowl often with a rubber spatula, until the batter is smooth. Spread evenly in the prepared pans.

Bake until the tops spring back when lightly pressed and a toothpick inserted in the centers comes out clean, 25 to 30 minutes. Cool for 10 minutes on wire cake racks. Invert the cakes and unmold onto the racks. Turn right side up and cool completely.

To make the frosting: In a liquid measuring cup, mix the milk, chocolate syrup, dissolved coffee, and vanilla until combined. Sift the confectioners' sugar and cocoa into a medium bowl and add the butter. Using an electric mixer at low speed, beat until crumbly. Gradually add enough of the chocolate milk to make a spreadable frosting (you may not need all of the milk mixture).

Place a dab of frosting in the center of the serving plate. Place one layer, upside down, on the plate. Spread with about ½ cup of frosting. Place the remaining cake layer, right side up, on the bottom layer. Frost the top, then the sides, with the remaining frosting. If serving later, refrigerate until the frosting sets, then loosely cover with plastic wrap. Return to room temperature before serving.

Pineapple Upside-Down Cake

It's best to make pineapple upside-down cake in a cast-iron skillet, but other 10-inch skillets work, too. If your skillet has a plastic handle, wrap the handle in a double thickness of aluminum foil to protect it from melting in the oven.

Makes 6 to 8 servings

Two 8-ounce cans sliced pineapple in heavy syrup
8 tablespoons (1 stick) butter
¾ cup plus ⅓ cup granulated sugar
⅓ cup packed light brown sugar
8 maraschino cherries
1 cup cake flour (not self-rising cake flour)
1½ teaspoons baking powder
½ teaspoon salt
¼ cup butter-flavored or plain vegetable shortening
½ cup half-and-half
1 large egg, at room temperature
2 teaspoons vanilla extract
Grated zest of ½ lemon

Preheat the oven to 350°F. Drain the pineapple well, reserving 3 tablespoons of the syrup. Pat the pineapple slices dry with paper towels.

In a 10-inch skillet, preferably cast-iron or nonstick, melt the butter over medium heat. Stir in ⅓ cup of the granulated sugar and the brown sugar. Cook, stirring often, until well blended, about 2 minutes. Remove from the heat. Arrange 8 pineapple rings in the hot sugar mixture—7 slices around the edges, and 1 in the center (you may have to squeeze them in, but they'll fit). Place 1 maraschino cherry in the center of each ring.

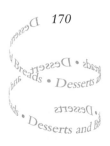

Sift the flour, baking powder, and salt together. Set aside. In a medium bowl, using an electric mixer at high speed, beat the vegetable shortening and remaining ¾ cup of the granulated sugar until well combined and crumbly, about 1 minute. Beat in the reserved 3 tablespoons of pineapple juice, the half-and-half, egg, vanilla, and lemon zest. With the mixer on low speed, beat in the flour mixture to make a smooth batter. Pour evenly over the pineapple.

Bake until the cake pulls away from the sides of the pan and the top is golden brown, about 35 minutes. Cool on a wire cake rack for 5 minutes. Carefully invert onto a serving plate (the syrup is hot!), fruit side up. Serve warm or cool to room temperature.

Anna's Irresistible Pound Cake

My mother-in-law's recipe is the perfect "plain" cake. It's delicious on its own with a glass of milk, but it is really great "shortcake-style," with some sliced peaches and strawberries.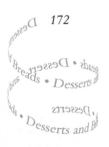

Makes 12 servings

4 cups cake flour (not self-rising cake flour)
2 teaspoons baking powder
1¼ cups milk
2 teaspoons vanilla extract
Grated zest of 1 lemon or 1½ teaspoons lemon
    extract
2 cups (4 sticks) butter, at room temperature
2½ cups sugar
6 large eggs, at room temperature

Preheat the oven to 350°F. Butter and flour a 10-inch tube pan, tapping out the excess flour.

Sift the flour and baking powder into a medium bowl. In a glass measuring cup, combine the milk, vanilla, and lemon zest.

In a large bowl, using an electric mixer at high speed, beat the butter until creamy, about 1 minute. Gradually add the sugar and beat until light in color and texture, about 2 minutes. One at a time, beat in the eggs. In three additions, beat in the flour mixture, alternating with the milk mixture. Beat until smooth, scraping down the sides of the bowl with a rubber spatula as needed. Pour into the prepared pan and smooth the top.

Bake until a toothpick inserted in the center of the cake comes out clean, about 1 hour, 15 minutes. Cool on a wire cake rack for 10 minutes. Run a sharp knife around the sides and tube section of the pan and lift off the pan. Slide the knife under the cake to release it from the tube section. Cool completely on the cake rack. Remove the cake from the tube section. Wrap tightly with plastic wrap until ready to serve.

My nephew Michael, Zuri, and Armstead trying to sweet talk my mother-in-law into making her famous pound cake.

Scandalously Rich Rum Cake

CAKE

1 cup finely chopped walnuts or pecans
One 18½-ounce package yellow cake mix
One 3¾-ounce package instant vanilla pudding mix
4 large eggs, at room temperature
½ cup water
½ cup vegetable oil
½ cup dark rum

GLAZE

8 tablespoons (1 stick) butter
1 cup sugar
¼ cup water
½ cup dark rum

Preheat the oven to 350°F. Butter well a 10-inch nonstick fluted tube (Bundt) pan. Sprinkle the nuts inside the pan, trying to coat the sides as much as possible. Let any stray nuts collect in the bottom of the pan.

To make the cake: In a medium bowl, using an electric mixer at low speed, combine the cake mix, pudding mix, eggs, water, oil, and rum, scraping down the sides of the bowl as needed, until smooth. Pour into the prepared pan and smooth the top.

Bake until a toothpick inserted in the center of the cake comes out clean, 50 to 60 minutes. Cool on a wire cake rack for 10 minutes. Invert and unmold the cake onto the rack and let cool until warm, about 30 minutes.

Meanwhile, make the glaze: In a medium saucepan, melt the butter over medium heat. Stir in the sugar and water and bring to a boil. Cook for 5 minutes. Remove from the heat and stir in the rum.

Place the cake, upside down, onto a serving platter. Pierce the cake all over with a toothpick. Drizzle and brush about one-third of the glaze over the bottom of the cake. Turn the cake over. Brush the remaining glaze all over the sides and top of the cake. Be patient while the cake soaks up the glaze. The entire glazing could take about 5 minutes. Cool the cake completely before serving.

Patti's Pointers: The nuts should be finely chopped. A food processor works well, but be careful not to process them into nut butter.

Be patient as you brush and drizzle the rum glaze over the cake. It takes time for the cake to soak up the glaze.

Cinnamon and Pecan Coffee Cake

This coffee cake can be made a day ahead, wrapped in plastic wrap, and stored at room temperature, or served warm out of the oven. Either way, it will fill the kitchen with spicy aromas that will make your mouth water. One tip: Even if your fluted cake pan is nonstick, it's a good idea to butter and flour it anyway.

Makes 12 servings

1 cup (2 sticks) butter, at room temperature
1 cup plus 1½ teaspoons granulated sugar
½ cup packed light brown sugar
2 large eggs, at room temperature
½ teaspoon vanilla extract
2 cups all-purpose flour
1 teaspoon baking powder
½ teaspoon baking soda
¼ teaspoon salt
1 cup sour cream
½ cup (2 ounces) chopped walnuts
½ cup (2 ounces) chopped pecans
2 teaspoons ground cinnamon
½ teaspoon ground nutmeg

Preheat the oven to 350°F. Lightly butter and flour a nonstick 10-inch fluted tube (Bundt) pan.

In a medium bowl, using an electric mixer at high speed, beat the butter, 1 cup of the granulated sugar, and the brown sugar until light in color and texture, about 2 minutes. One at a time, beat in the eggs, then the vanilla.

Sift the flour, baking powder, baking soda, and salt together. In three additions, with the mixer at low speed, beat the flour mixture into the butter mix-

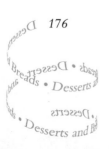

ture, alternating with the sour cream. Beat until smooth, scraping down the sides of the bowl with a rubber spatula.

In a small bowl, mix the walnuts, pecans, cinnamon, and nutmeg. Spread one-third of the batter into the prepared pan. Sprinkle with half of the chopped nut mixture. Top with half of the remaining batter, spreading the batter to cover the nuts. Sprinkle with the remaining nuts, then spread with the remaining batter and smooth the top.

Bake until a toothpick inserted in the center of the cake comes out clean, about 1 hour. Cool on a wire cake rack for 10 minutes. Invert onto the cake rack. Serve warm or cool completely and serve at room temperature.

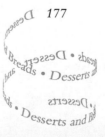

Aunt Hattie's Scrumptious Sweet Tater Bread

Like so many of my special recipes, my Aunt Hattie Mae gave me this one. It has only been in recent years that I've gotten into baking and, so much of what I know about it I learned from Aunt Hattie and Aunt Josh. They taught me about baking the perfect quick bread, for example. Mix the flour into a batter by hand, or on low speed if using a mixer (my aunts would never use a mixer) to ensure you won't overmix it. And, to prevent crumbling, don't slice the bread until it has cooled completely.

The high priestesses of cooking: Aunt Joshia Mae and Aunt Hattie Mae.

In the ten years since I lost my father to Alzheimer's disease, Aunt Hattie and Aunt Josh have nurtured me not only with their cooking, but with cherished family stories. Thanks to them, I know why cooking is in my blood. I can't count the hours I've sat with them at the kitchen table as they told me about the past—Grandmother Tempie's garden where she grew collards, okra, and tomatoes the color of rubies. The time she and her neighbor Miss Lil almost came to blows over whose tomatoes were the biggest. Grandmother Mariah's melt-in-your-mouth mullet fish which she fried, along with her famous hush puppies, in the big black wash pot. Daddy's dreams, from the time he was a little boy, of one day opening a restaurant.

Aunt Hattie and Aunt Josh are some cooking Sisters themselves. In Georgia, the ancestral home of my father's family, their culinary skill is legendary. For years, Aunt Hattie and Aunt Josh cooked in private homes for wealthy White families. More than a few folks stopped speaking to each other after one family

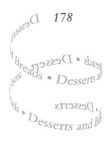

visited another for dinner and an awestruck diner tried to hire Auntie Hattie or Aunt Josh away.

Aunt Josh even cooked President Eisenhower his first soul food meal. He'd spent the night with the family she was working for and, the next morning, Aunt Josh rose with the sun and cooked him a soul food banquet: hogshead bacon, sausage scrapple, grits and redeye gravy, sweet potato waffles, and, of course, Grandmother Tempie's flying biscuits. Aunt Josh says President Eisenhower mopped his plate clean. Can't you just see the look on the face of the White House chef when Ike got back to Washington and asked him to whip up some grits and gravy!!?

Aunt Josh and Aunt Hattie are both fabulous cooks, and as much as I relish their food, the stories they have told me over the years about our family are what I love most. When you put Aunt Hattie's Scrumptious Sweet Tater Bread in the oven, invite a very old or very young relative to join you in the kitchen. While it's baking, listen to or pass on your own family's very special legends and lore. You'll be glad you did.

2 medium orange-fleshed sweet potatoes (about
   1½ pounds)
8 tablespoons (1 stick) butter, at room temperature
1 cup sugar
2 large eggs, at room temperature
½ cup evaporated milk
½ teaspoon vanilla extract
Grated zest of ½ lemon or ⅛ teaspoon lemon
   extract
2 cups all-purpose flour
1 teaspoon baking soda
¼ teaspoon salt

Preheat the oven to 350°F. Butter and flour a 9 × 5 × 3-inch loaf pan, tapping out the excess flour.

Bring a large saucepan of lightly salted water to a boil over high heat. Add the sweet potatoes and cook until tender, about 25 minutes. Drain, and rinse under cold water until easy to handle. Peel the sweet potatoes, place in a medium bowl, and mash well. Measure 1 cup mashed sweet potatoes, saving the remaining sweet potatoes for another purpose. In a large bowl, using a handheld electric mixer on high speed, beat the butter and sugar until combined, about 1 minute. One at a time, beat in the eggs. Beat in the sweet potatoes, evaporated milk, vanilla, and lemon zest. In a medium bowl, mix the flour, baking soda, and salt. With the mixer on low speed, gradually beat the flour mixture into the sweet potato mixture, scraping down the sides of the bowl with a rubber spatula. Spread evenly in the prepared pan.

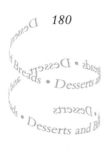

Bake until the top springs back when lightly pressed and a toothpick inserted in the center comes out clean, about 1 hour, 15 minutes. Cool for 10 minutes on a wire rack. Invert onto the wire rack, turn right side up, and cool completely.

Best-Ever Banana Bread: Substitute 1 cup mashed ripe bananas for the mashed sweet potatoes. Reduce baking time to 1 hour.

Pecan Butterscotch Blondie Bars

Makes about 12 bars

12 tablespoons (1½ sticks) butter, at room
    temperature
⅓ cup granulated sugar
⅓ cup packed light brown sugar
1 large egg
1 teaspoon vanilla extract
1¼ cups self-rising flour
¾ cup (3 ounces) finely chopped pecans

Preheat the oven to 350°F. Lightly butter a 10½ × 7 × 1½-inch baking pan.

In a medium bowl, using an electric mixer at high speed, beat the butter until creamy, about 1 minute. Add the granulated and brown sugars and beat until light and fluffy, about 2 minutes. Beat in the egg and vanilla. Using a wooden spoon, stir in the flour, then the pecans. Spread evenly in the prepared pan.

Bake until a toothpick inserted in the center comes out clean, about 25 minutes. Cool in the pan on a wire cake rack. Cut into 12 bars and remove from the pan.

Patti's Pointers: My Aunt Joshia Mae gave me this recipe and, as she explained to me, this is not a crisp cookie, but a soft, chewy vanilla-y bar. If you want a quick icing for these bars, sprinkle 1 cup (6 ounces) peanut butter, butterscotch, or semisweet or milk chocolate chips over the hot bars (still in the pan), as soon as they come out of the oven. Let stand until the chips soften, about 5 minutes, then spread evenly over the top. As the bars cool, the chips will make a thin icing.

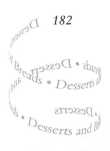

Peanut Butter Cookies

Taste these soft, chewy peanut butter cookies, and if you can eat just one, you're a stronger person than I am. It's worth going out and buying a cookie jar just to hold them.

Makes about 32 cookies

½ cup peanut butter
¼ cup vegetable shortening
4 tablespoons (½ stick) butter, at room temperature
½ cup granulated sugar
½ cup packed light brown sugar
2 large eggs
1½ cups self-rising flour

Position the racks in the top third and center of the oven and preheat to 375°F. Lightly grease 2 cookie sheets.

In a large bowl, using an electric mixer at high speed, beat the peanut butter, shortening, and butter until well combined, about 1 minute. Add the granulated and brown sugars and beat until light and fluffy, about 2 minutes. Beat in the eggs. Using a wooden spoon, stir in the flour.

Using about 1 tablespoon of dough for each, form the dough into balls. Place the balls about 2 inches apart on the prepared cookie sheets. Using a fork, flatten each ball of dough with a crosshatch pattern.

Bake, switching the position of the sheets from top to bottom halfway through baking, until the cookies are lightly browned around the edges, 12 to 15 minutes. Let cool on the pan for 1 minute, then transfer to wire cake racks to cool completely.

Basic Piecrust

Makes one 9-inch piecrust

1½ cups all-purpose flour
½ teaspoon salt
½ cup butter-flavored vegetable shortening, chilled
⅓ cup ice water

Sift the flour and salt into a medium bowl. Add the shortening. Using a fork or a pastry blender, cut the shortening into the flour until the mixture resembles coarse crumbs with a few pea-sized bits. Stirring with the fork, gradually add enough of the water until the mixture clumps together (you may need more or less water). Gather up the dough and press into a thick disk. If desired, wrap the dough in wax paper and refrigerate for up to 1 hour.

Basic Piecrust for Double-Crust Pie: Following the instructions above, use 2 cups all-purpose flour, ¾ teaspoon salt, ⅔ cup butter-flavored vegetable shortening, and ½ cup ice water. Divide the dough into 2 thick disks, in one-third and two-third portions. If desired, wrap each disk in wax paper and refrigerate for up to 1 hour.

Patti's Pointers: If you want a tender, flaky piecrust, you have to use shortening. Some cooks make their dough with butter because they like the flavor, but it bakes into a crumbly crust—and with most pie lovers, flaky is the name of the game. My solution is to use butter-flavored Crisco.

Like biscuits, piecrust shouldn't be overworked. Handle with care. Chilled vegetable shortening and water will also help piecrust stay nice and flaky.

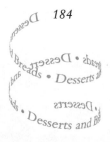

Decadent and Delicious Pecan Pie

Makes 8 servings

Basic Piecrust (page 184)
1½ cups (about 6 ounces) whole pecans
1 cup sugar
1 cup light corn syrup
3 large eggs
2 tablespoons butter, melted
1 teaspoon vanilla extract
¼ teaspoon salt
Vanilla ice cream or whipped cream

Preheat the oven to 350°F. On a lightly floured work surface, roll out the dough into a 13-inch circle about ⅛ inch thick. Fold the dough in half. Transfer to a 9-inch pie pan, and gently unfold the dough to fit into the pan. Using scissors or a sharp knife, trim the excess dough to a 1-inch overhang. Fold the dough under itself so the edge of the fold is flush with the edge of the pan. Flute the dough around the edge of the pan. Spread the pecans in the pie shell.

In a medium bowl, using an electric mixer at low speed, beat the sugar, corn syrup, eggs, melted butter, vanilla, and salt until well combined. Pour into the pie shell.

Bake until a knife inserted in the center of the pie comes out clean, about 1¼ hours. Cool on a wire cake rack at least 1 hour before serving. Serve warm or at room temperature, with the ice cream.

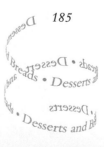

Amazing Apple-Butterscotch Pie

Makes 8 servings

Basic Piecrust for a Double-Crust Pie (page 184)
1 cup packed light brown sugar
¼ cup half-and-half
5 tablespoons unsalted butter
1 teaspoon vanilla extract
7 medium Granny Smith apples, peeled, cored, and
   cut into ¼-inch wedges
1 tablespoon fresh lemon juice
3 tablespoons cornstarch
Grated zest of ½ lemon
Grated zest of ¼ orange, optional
½ teaspoon ground cinnamon
¼ teaspoon ground allspice
¼ teaspoon ground nutmeg
1 teaspoon all-purpose flour

Preheat the oven to 375°F.

In a small saucepan, stir ¾ cup of the brown sugar and the half-and-half over medium heat until the sugar dissolves. Remove from the heat and add the butter and the vanilla. Stir until the butter melts. Set the butterscotch mixture aside to cool completely.

In a medium bowl, toss the apples with the lemon juice. Add the remaining ¼ cup brown sugar, the cornstarch, lemon zest, and the orange zest (if using), cinnamon, allspice, and nutmeg.

On a lightly floured work surface, roll out the larger disk of dough into a 13-inch round about ⅛ inch thick. Fold the dough in half. Transfer to a 9-inch pie pan, and gently unfold the dough to fit into the pan. Sprinkle the bottom of the

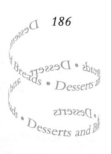

dough with the flour. Fill the pie pan with the apple mixture. Pour the cooled butterscotch mixture over the apples.

On a lightly floured work surface, roll out the remaining pie dough into a 10- to 11-inch round about ⅛ inch thick. Fold the dough in half, and gently unfold over the apples to cover the filling. Using scissors or a sharp knife, trim the edges of the 2 piecrusts to a 1-inch overhang. Pinching the 2 crusts together, fold the dough under itself so the edge of the fold is flush with the edge of the pie pan. Flute the crust around the edges of the pan. Cut a few slits in the top crust so the steam can escape.

Bake until golden brown and the juices are bubbling (look into the slits to check), about 45 minutes. Cool completely on a wire cake rack.

Patti's Pointers: This recipe is a little different (and more luscious) than other apple pies thanks to its creamy butterscotch filling. Sprinkle a bit of flour on the bottom crust to keep it from getting soggy.

Showing off my first apple butterscotch pie to my son Dodd and friend Lennie.

Banana and Toasted Almond Cream Pie

Makes 8 servings

Basic Piecrust (page 184)
⅓ cup (about 1½ ounces) sliced almonds
⅔ cup granulated sugar
¼ cup cornstarch
¼ teaspoon salt
2½ cups half-and-half
3 large egg yolks, beaten
¾ teaspoon vanilla extract
¾ teaspoon almond extract
2 medium bananas, thinly sliced
1 cup heavy cream
2 tablespoons confectioners' sugar

Preheat the oven to 400°F. On a lightly floured work surface, roll out the dough into a 13-inch round about ⅛ inch thick. Fold the dough in half. Transfer to a 9-inch pie pan, and gently unfold the dough to fit into the pan. Using scissors or a sharp knife, trim the dough to a 1-inch overhang. Fold the dough under itself so the edge of the fold is flush with the edge of the pan. Flute the dough around the edge of the pan. Pierce the dough a few times with a fork.

Bake, piercing the dough with a fork if it puffs up during baking, until the dough is golden brown, about 20 minutes. Cool completely on a wire cake rack. Reduce the oven temperature to 375°F.

Spread the almonds on a baking sheet. Bake, stirring occasionally, until lightly toasted, 8 to 10 minutes. Transfer to a plate and cool completely.

Meanwhile, in a medium, heavy-bottomed saucepan, mix ⅔ cup of the sugar, the cornstarch, and salt. Gradually stir in about ½ cup of the half-and-half to dissolve the cornstarch. Stir in the remaining 2 cups half-and-half and the egg yolks.

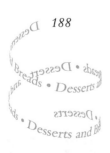

Stirring constantly with a wooden spatula, bring to a boil over medium heat. Reduce the heat to medium-low and boil, stirring constantly, for 1 minute. Remove from the heat. Stir in ½ teaspoon each of the vanilla and almond extracts. Press a piece of plastic wrap directly on the surface of the filling. Pierce a few holes in the wrap with the tip of a knife to let the steam escape. Cool on a wire cake rack for 30 minutes.

Spread about ¹/₂ cup of the filling in the pie shell. Cover with the banana slices, then spread with the remaining filling. Cover the filling with another piece of plastic wrap and let cool completely.

In a chilled medium bowl, using an electric mixer on high speed, beat the cream, confectioners' sugar, and the remaining ¼ teaspoon each vanilla and almond extracts just until stiff. Remove the plastic wrap, and spread over the filling. Sprinkle with the toasted almonds. Refrigerate until ready to serve. Serve chilled.

Banana Cream Meringue Pie: Delete the whipped cream and toasted almond topping. Separate 3 large eggs. Use the yolks in the filling as directed. To make the meringue, use the whites and ¼ cup sugar, as directed in Citrus Meringue Pie on page 190. Spread the meringue over the filling and bake in a preheated 375°F oven until lightly browned, 8 to 10 minutes.

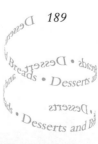

Citrus Meringue Pie

It's pretty safe to state that everyone loves meringue pie. I use three kinds of zest in the filling to give it more citrus-y flavor and top it with a generous heap of meringue. The secret of a meringue that doesn't shrink? Spread the meringue onto *warm* filling, and be sure it is touching, and anchored to, the crust.

Makes 8 servings

Basic Piecrust (page 184)
1⅓ cups sugar
¼ cup cornstarch
1½ cups water
4 large eggs, separated
¼ cup fresh lemon juice
1 tablespoon butter
Grated zest of 1 lemon
Grated zest of ½ orange
Grated zest of ½ lime

Preheat the oven to 400°F. On a lightly floured work surface, roll out the dough until it is about 13 inches in diameter and ⅛ inch thick. Fold the dough in half. Transfer to a 9-inch pie pan, and gently unfold the dough to fit into the pan. Trim the overhanging dough to extend 1 inch beyond the edge of the pan. Fold the excess dough under so the edge of the dough is flush with the edge of the pan. Flute the dough around the edge of the pan. Pierce the dough a few times with a fork.

Bake, piercing the dough with a fork if it puffs up during baking, until the crust is golden brown, about 20 minutes. Set aside on a wire cake rack (the pie shell doesn't have to cool completely). Reduce the oven temperature to 375°F.

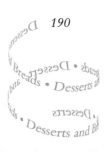

Meanwhile, in a medium, heavy-bottomed saucepan, stir 1 cup sugar with the cornstarch. Gradually stir in about ½ cup of the water to dissolve the cornstarch. Add the remaining 1 cup water. In a small bowl, beat the yolks and stir into the cornstarch mixture. Stirring constantly with a wooden spatula, bring to a boil over medium heat. Reduce the heat to medium-low and boil, stirring constantly, for 1 minute. Remove from the heat. Stir in the lemon juice, butter, and lemon, orange, and lime zests. Spread the warm filling into the pastry shell.

In a clean medium bowl, using an electric mixer on high speed, beat the egg whites until foamy. Gradually beat in the remaining ⅓ cup sugar until the whites are stiff and glossy. Spread over the warm filling, being sure that the meringue touches the piecrust.

Bake until the meringue is lightly browned, 8 to 10 minutes. Cool completely on the wire cake rack. Refrigerate until ready to serve. Serve chilled.

Homemade pies cooling on the stove.

Wicked Peach Cobbler

Every baker has very strong opinions on how to make a cobbler. Some prefer a biscuit topping, others swear by a piecrust. This cook is from the pastry school of thought, and even adds a layer in the middle of the peach filling that cooks up like a noodle and lightly thickens the fruit juices. This is a basic recipe that acts as a blueprint for other cobblers. Substitute 6 cups of blueberries or blackberries, or peeled and sliced nectarines, apples, or pears. Frozen fruit is fine, too.

Makes 4 to 6 servings

Basic Piecrust for Double-Crust Pie (page 184)
3 pounds medium peaches, peeled, pitted, and cut
    into ¼-inch slices
2 tablespoons cornstarch
1 cup sugar
2 teaspoons fresh lemon juice
½ teaspoon ground cinnamon, plus more for the
    top of the crust
4 tablespoons (½ stick) butter, chilled, cut into small
    pieces

Preheat the oven to 375°F. Lightly butter an 8-inch square baking dish.

In a medium bowl, toss the peaches, cornstarch, sugar, lemon juice, and cinnamon. Fold in the butter. Spoon half of the peach mixture into the prepared dish.

On a lightly floured work surface, roll out the smaller disk of dough into an 8-inch square about ⅛ inch thick, trimming the dough as needed. Place over the peaches in the baking dish. Top with the remaining peaches. Roll out the larger disk of dough into an 11-inch square about ⅛ inch thick, trimming as needed. Fit over the top of the baking dish, letting the dough hang down the sides of the dish. Pinch the dough firmly onto the top edge of the dish. Press the overhanging dough onto the sides of the dish. Cut a few slits in the top of the dough. Place the dish on a baking sheet to catch any drips.

Bake until the fruit juices are bubbling and the top is golden brown, about 40 minutes. Sprinkle the top of the dough with cinnamon. Serve hot, warm, or at room temperature.

Showing off my peach cobbler before I put it in the oven.

Norma's Black-Bottom Sweet Potato Pie

Norma's sweet potato pie has a thin layer of brown sugar on the bottom crust. Not only does this "black bottom" give flavor, it helps keep the filling from making the crust soggy. Her recipe makes a good amount of the delicious filling—this isn't one of those skimpy sweet potato pies. It tastes like sweet potatoes, not pineapple or raisins or other fillers that some people stick in their pies. Serve it with whipped cream, if you wish.

Makes 8 servings

Basic Piecrust (page 184)
3 large orange-fleshed sweet potatoes (Louisiana yams), scrubbed
8 tablespoons (1 stick) butter, melted
¾ cup packed light brown sugar
½ cup granulated sugar
2 large eggs, beaten
¼ cup half-and-half
¾ teaspoon ground cinnamon
1 teaspoon ground nutmeg

On a lightly floured work surface, roll out the dough into a 13-inch circle about ⅛ inch thick. Fold the dough in half. Transfer to a 9-inch pie pan, and gently unfold the dough to fit into the pan. Using scissors or a sharp knife, trim the dough to a 1-inch overhang. Fold the dough under itself so the edge of the fold is flush with the edge of the pan. Flute the dough around the edge of the pan. Cover with plastic wrap and refrigerate while making the filling.

Bring a large pot of lightly salted water to a boil over high heat. Add the sweet potatoes and reduce the heat to medium. Cook until the sweet potatoes are tender when pierced with a knife, about 30 minutes. Drain and run under cold water

until cool enough to handle. Peel the sweet potatoes and place in a medium bowl. Mash with an electric mixer on medium speed until very smooth. Measure 3 cups mashed sweet potatoes, keeping any extra for another use, and set aside.

Preheat the oven to 400°F. Uncover the pie shell and brush the interior with some of the melted butter. Sprinkle ¼ cup of the brown sugar over the bottom of the pie shell. Bake until the pie dough is set and just beginning to brown, about 15 minutes. If the pie shell puffs, do not prick it.

Meanwhile, in a medium bowl, using an electric mixer on low speed, mix the mashed sweet potatoes, the remaining melted butter and ½ cup brown sugar, the granulated sugar, eggs, half-and-half, cinnamon, and nutmeg. Spread into the partially baked pie shell, smoothing the top.

Reduce the oven temperature to 350°F. Bake until a knife inserted in the center of the filling comes out clean, about 1½ hours. Cool completely on a wire cake rack. Cover and refrigerate until ready to serve.

My best friend, Norma, and me stirring it up in Norma's kitchen.

Aunt Joshia Mae's Blackberry Doobie

Blackberries with dumplings—that's all that there is to a doobie. It shares a place in the dessert hall of fame with other fruit desserts with funny names like grunt, slump, and pandowdy. This is a good hot-weather dessert because you don't have to turn on the oven. You can use blueberries or a combination of berries but just don't use strawberries—they get pale when cooked. You can also use frozen berries.

Makes 6 to 8 servings

4 pints fresh blackberries or blueberries
¾ cup sugar
½ cup water
4 tablespoons (½ stick) butter, cut into pieces
2 tablespoons cornstarch dissolved in ¼ cup water

DUMPLINGS

2 cups self-rising flour
2 tablespoons sugar
½ cup vegetable shortening
⅔ cup milk

In a deep 12-inch skillet, toss the berries, sugar, water, and butter. Bring to a simmer over medium heat, stirring often. Reduce the heat to low and simmer for 5 minutes. Stir in the dissolved cornstarch and cook until the juices thicken, about 1 minute.

Meanwhile, make the dumplings: In a medium bowl, mix the flour and sugar. Add the shortening. Using a fork or a pastry blender, cut the shortening into the flour until the mixture resembles coarse crumbs. Using a fork, stir in the milk.

Using a scant tablespoon of dough for each dumpling, roll into 24 balls and place on a baking sheet.

Drop the dumplings into the simmering berries. Cover tightly and cook until the dumplings are cooked through, about 20 minutes. Serve hot, spooned into individual bowls.

Baby Henry's Bread Pudding

My father, Henry Holte, Jr., was known all over Georgia for his bread pudding. It wasn't just his signature dish, it was his art. Daddy's bread pudding was so good, in fact, when he opened his restaurant, Baby Henry's Place, back home in Georgia, his customers insisted that he make it every single day, no exceptions, no excuses. The first time I tasted it, I understood why. Sweet and satisfying, Daddy's bread pudding is old-fashioned comfort food at its very best. Eat some and I promise: You'll understand exactly how comfort food got its name.

Makes **4 to 6** servings

4 cups stale, firm white sliced sandwich bread, cut
   into 1-inch squares (about 7 ounces)
3 cups milk
3 large eggs
1½ cups sugar
2 teaspoons vanilla extract
¼ teaspoon ground cinnamon
12 tablespoons (1½ sticks) butter, melted
½ cup raisins

Preheat the oven to 350°F. Lightly butter a 12 × 8-inch (2½-quart) baking dish.

In a large bowl, gently mix the bread and milk. Let stand for 5 minutes.

In another large bowl, mix the eggs, sugar, vanilla, and cinnamon. Gradually stir in the melted butter. Add the bread with its milk and the raisins, and mix gently. Pour into the prepared dish.

Bake until golden brown and a knife inserted in the center comes out clean, about 45 minutes. Cool for 10 minutes. Serve hot, warm, or at room temperature.

Patti's Pointers: Fresh bread makes soggy bread pudding. With all of the preservatives they put into bread these days, it's hard to get bread to go stale. (All of a sudden it just tastes and smells bad.) It's best to spread the bread on the kitchen counter and let it stand for a few hours or overnight, uncovered, to dry out.

Really Good Rice Pudding

Makes 4 to 6 servings

2 large eggs
½ cup sugar
2 cups milk
2 cups half-and-half
1 teaspoon vanilla extract
¼ teaspoon ground cinnamon
⅛ teaspoon ground nutmeg
½ cup uncooked long-grain rice
½ cup raisins
2 tablespoons butter, chilled, cut into small pieces

Preheat the oven to 300°F. Lightly butter an 8 × 11½-inch (2-quart) baking dish.

In a medium bowl, beat the eggs and sugar until combined. Beat in the milk, half-and-half, vanilla, cinnamon, and nutmeg. Stir in the rice and raisins. Pour into the prepared dish. Dot the top with the butter.

Bake, stirring well every 30 minutes, until the pudding is set and the top is lightly browned, about 2 hours. Serve warm or at room temperature.

Patti's Pointers: Patience is a virtue, but even more so when you're making rice pudding. The rice takes its sweet time as it softens up. The pudding needs to be stirred occasionally to combine the cooked rice around the edges with the less-cooked rice in the center. If you refrigerate the pudding, let it stand out for about a half hour before serving—chilled rice is hard, and needs to warm and soften up a little.

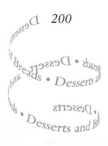

Grandmother Tempie's Flying Biscuits

Makes 8 biscuits

2 cups all-purpose flour
1 tablespoon baking powder
¼ teaspoon sugar
½ teaspoon salt
½ cup vegetable shortening
¾ cup buttermilk

Preheat the oven to 425°F.

Sift the flour, baking powder, sugar, and salt into a bowl. Add the shortening. Using a fork or pastry blender, cut the shortening into the flour mixture until it resembles fine crumbs. Stir in the buttermilk to make a soft dough.

Place the dough on a lightly floured work surface and knead gently, just until the surface of the dough isn't sticky. Do not overknead. Pat into a thick disk. Cut the dough into 8 pieces. Roll and pat each piece of dough into a 2½-inch round biscuit about ½ inch thick. Place the biscuits 1 inch apart on an ungreased baking sheet.

Bake until golden brown, 18 to 20 minutes. Serve hot.

Patti's Pointers: As my Grandmother Tempie knew, the secret to a light biscuit is tender loving care. Don't overhandle the dough or the biscuits will bake up tough. There are three points in the recipe when you may want to use some elbow grease, but hold back:

1. Stir the dough just until it is moistened and clumps together.
2. Gather up the dough and knead it just a couple of times until it smooths out.
3. Use a gentle hand when you form the biscuits.

Sweet Potato 'n' Spice Waffles

Makes **sixteen** 4-inch square waffles

1 large sweet potato (about 14 ounces)
Nonstick vegetable oil spray
2¼ cups all-purpose flour
4 teaspoons baking powder
1½ teaspoons ground cinnamon
¼ teaspoon ground nutmeg
½ teaspoon salt
1 cup milk
1 cup half-and-half
¼ cup packed light brown sugar
4 large eggs, separated
4 tablespoons (½ stick) butter, melted
Softened butter and warm maple syrup

Bring a large pot of lightly salted water to a boil over high heat. Add the sweet potato and reduce the heat to medium. Cook until the sweet potato is tender when pierced with the tip of a knife, 30 to 40 minutes. Drain and run under cold water until cool enough to handle. Peel and mash the sweet potato. Measure out 1 cup mashed sweet potato, using any excess for another purpose.

Preheat the oven to 200°F. Preheat a waffle iron according to the manufacturer's instructions. Spray the grids with nonstick vegetable spray.

Meanwhile, in a large bowl, mix the flour, baking powder, cinnamon, nutmeg, and salt. In a medium bowl, using a whisk or a large spoon, mix the reserved mashed sweet potatoes with the milk, half-and-half, brown sugar, and egg yolks until well combined and the sugar dissolves. Pour into the dry ingredients and mix until the batter is moistened, but still lumpy. Using a rubber spatula, fold in the melted butter—the batter should still be almost, but not quite, smooth.

In a clean medium bowl, using an electric mixer at high speed, beat the egg whites just until stiff peaks form; do not overbeat. Stir about one-fourth of the egg whites into the batter to lighten. Using the spatula, fold in the remaining egg whites until the batter is smooth.

Pour a generous 1 cup of the batter into the center of the open waffle iron grid. Close the waffle iron. Cook until the waffle iron indicator shows that the waffle is done (or the waffle is crisp and golden brown), 6 to 7 minutes. Keep the waffles warm in the oven while preparing the remaining waffles. Serve hot, with butter and maple syrup.

Patti's Pointers: Like biscuits and piecrust, for the most tender waffles, don't overbeat the batter. When combining the moist and dry ingredients, stir them just until moistened—the batter should be lumpy. When you fold in the butter, the lumps will dissipate, but not entirely. Not until the beaten egg whites have been folded in should the batter finally become smooth. If you already have the mashed sweet potatoes, you can make the batter while the waffle iron heats up.

Beyond-Good Bacon and Buttermilk Corn Bread

This is a rich, cakelike, tender corn bread. I don't serve any of that hard, thin, crumbly corn bread.

If the cook prefers, delete the bacon, and substitute 3 tablespoons melted butter for the bacon drippings.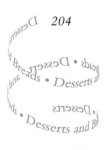

Makes 9 servings

6 strips bacon
1 cup buttermilk
One 8½-ounce can creamed corn
1 large egg
1 cup white or yellow cornmeal
1 cup all-purpose flour
3 tablespoons sugar
2 teaspoons baking powder
½ teaspoon baking soda
½ teaspoon salt
1 cup fresh or thawed frozen corn kernels (see
   Note, page 18)

Preheat the oven to 400°F. Grease well an 8-inch square baking pan.

In a large skillet, cook the bacon over medium heat until crisp and brown. Transfer the bacon to paper towels to drain and cool, reserving the drippings in the skillet.

Measure 3 tablespoons of the bacon drippings (add vegetable oil to the drippings, if necessary) into a small bowl. Add the buttermilk, creamed corn, and egg, and mix well.

In a medium bowl, mix the cornmeal, flour, sugar, baking powder, baking soda, and salt until well combined. Make a well in the center, and pour in the buttermilk mixture. Stir just until barely smooth—do not overbeat. Fold in the crumbled bacon and corn. Pour into the prepared pan and smooth the top.

Bake until the top is golden brown and springs back when pressed in the center, 30 to 35 minutes. Cool for 15 minutes before serving warm.

Sunday Supper Rolls

Fresh baked rolls right out of the oven—what a treat! These are often called "refrigerator rolls" because you can keep the dough in the refrigerator for a couple of days before baking. As a matter of fact, the dough gets better as it chills. Great bread bakers know that "old" dough makes the best bread. 🎼

Makes 1 dozen

1 cup hot tap water
¼ cup sugar
One ¼-ounce package active dry yeast
¼ cup vegetable shortening, melted and cooled to tepid
1 large egg
¾ teaspoon salt
3½ cups all-purpose flour, approximately
Melted butter, for brushing

In a large bowl, stir the hot water and sugar until the sugar dissolves. Let stand until tepid (100° to 110°F on an instant-read thermometer), about 10 minutes. Sprinkle the yeast into the bowl and let stand for 5 minutes. Stir to dissolve the yeast, then add the melted shortening, egg, and salt. Stir in enough flour to make a stiff dough, about 3 cups.

Turn the dough out onto a lightly floured work surface. Knead until smooth and elastic, about 10 minutes, adding more flour as necessary to keep the dough from sticking to the surface. Form the dough into a ball. Place in a well-greased medium bowl, and turn to coat the dough. Cover tightly with plastic wrap. Refrigerate until the dough doubles in volume, at least 8 hours and preferably overnight. (The dough can be refrigerated for up to 2 days. Punch down the dough every 12 hours or so.)

Punch down the dough. Lightly grease 12 muffin cups. Divide the dough into 12 pieces. Form each piece of dough into a taut ball, place in a prepared muffin cup, and press down the dough so it half-fills the cup. Cover loosely with plastic wrap. Let stand in a warm, draft-free place until the dough warms up and almost doubles in volume, about 1 hour.

Preheat the oven to 375°F. Brush the tops of the rolls with melted butter. Bake until golden brown, about 20 minutes. Serve warm or cool to room temperature.

Down-Home Hush Puppies

Makes about 20

1¼ cups all-purpose flour
1¼ cups white or yellow cornmeal
1½ teaspoons baking powder
¾ teaspoon salt
¼ teaspoon ground hot red (cayenne) pepper
1 cup milk
2 large eggs
1 small onion, finely chopped
Vegetable oil, for deep-frying

In a medium bowl, mix the flour, cornmeal, baking powder, salt, and red pepper. In a small bowl, beat the milk and eggs. Add to the dry ingredients with the onion. Stir just until combined.

In a large skillet, preferably cast-iron, add enough oil to come halfway up the sides. Heat over medium-high heat until very hot, but not smoking (365°F).

Using 1 tablespoon batter for each hush puppy, carefully drop the batter into the hot oil. Fry, turning once, until golden brown, about 4 minutes. Using a skimmer, transfer to paper towels to drain. Serve hot.

Patti's Pointers: Some families prefer the slightly sweeter flavor of white cornmeal. It's especially good in hush puppies. You can use yellow cornmeal, if you wish.

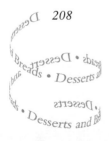

Index

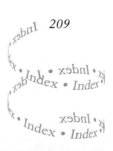

Index • Index • Index • Index • Index • Index • Index

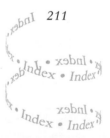

Index • Index • Index • Index • Index • Index • Index • Index

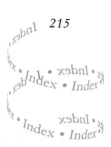

Index • Index • Index • Index • Index • Index • Index • Index •